PLOTINUS

ENNEAD V.5

THE *ENNEADS* OF PLOTINUS

With Philosophical Commentaries

Series Editors: John M. Dillon, Trinity College, Dublin and Andrew Smith, University College Dublin

TITLES FORTHCOMING IN THE SERIES INCLUDE:

Ennead I.6:
On Beauty
by Andrew Smith

Ennead II.4:
On Matter
by Anthony A. Long

Ennead II.5:
On What Exists Potentially and What Actually
by Cincia Arruzza

Ennead IV.3–4, 29:
Problems concerning the Soul
by John M. Dillon and Henry Blumenthal

Ennead IV.1–2, IV.4, 30–45 & IV.5:
Problems concerning the Soul
by Gary Gurtler

Ennead IV.7:
On the Immortality of the Soul
by Barrie Fleet

Ennead V.1:
On the Three Principial Hypostases
by Eric D. Perl

Ennead V.8:
On Intelligible Beauty
by Andrew Smith

Ennead VI.4 & VI.5:
On the Presence of Being, One and the Same, Everywhere
by Eyjólfur Emilsson and Steven Strange

Ennead VI.8:
On Free Will and the Will of the One
by Kevin Corrigan and John D. Turner

PLOTINUS
ENNEAD V.5

That the Intelligibles are not External to the Intellect, and on the Good

Translation with an Introduction and Commentary

LLOYD P. GERSON

PARMENIDES
PUBLISHING

Las Vegas | Zurich | Athens

PARMENIDES PUBLISHING
Las Vegas | Zurich | Athens

This edition published in 2013 by Parmenides Publishing
in the United States of America

ISBN soft cover: 978–1–930972–85–8
ISBN e-Book: 978–1–930972–86–5

Library of Congress Cataloging-in-Publication Data

Plotinus.
[Ennead. V, 5 English.]
Ennead V.5 : that the intelligibles are not external to the intellect, and on the good / Plotinus ; translation, with an introduction, and commentary, Lloyd P. Gerson.
pages cm. -- (The enneads of Plotinus with philosophical commentaries)
Includes index.
ISBN 978-1-930972-85-8 (pbk.) -- ISBN 978-1-930972-86-5 (e-book)
1. Plotinus. Ennead. V, 5. 2. Neoplatonism--Early works to 1800. 3. Soul--Early works to 1800. 4. One (The One in philosophy)--Early works to 1800. I. Gerson, Lloyd P. II. Title. III. Title: That the intelligibles are not external to the intellect, and on the good.
B693.E52E5 2013
186'.4--dc23
2013012315

Typeset in Janson Text and Palatino Linotype by Parmenides Publishing
Printed by Edwards Brothers Malloy, Ann Arbor, MI.

www.parmenides.com

Contents

To

Lillian

Julie

Henry

&

To the memory of Evelyn

Introduction to the Series With a Brief Outline of the Life and Thought of Plotinus (205–270 CE)

PLOTINUS WAS BORN IN 205 CE in Egypt of Greek-speaking parents. He attended the philosophical schools in Alexandria where he would have studied Plato (427–347 BCE), Aristotle (384–322 BCE), the Stoics and Epicureans as well as other Greek philosophical traditions. He began his serious philosophical education, however, relatively late in life, at the age of twenty-seven and was deeply impressed by the Platonist Ammonius Saccas about whom we, unfortunately, know very little, but with whom Plotinus studied for some eleven years. Even our knowledge of Plotinus' life is limited to what we can glean from Porphyry's introduction to his edition of his philosophical treatises, an account colored by Porphyry's own concerns. After completing his studies in Alexandria Plotinus attempted, by joining a military expedition of the Roman emperor Gordian III, to make contact with the

Brahmins in order to learn something of Indian thought. Unfortunately Gordian was defeated and killed (244). Plotinus somehow managed to extract himself and we next hear of him in Rome where he was able to set up a school of philosophy in the house of a high-ranking Roman lady by the name of Gemina. It is, perhaps, surprising that he had no formal contacts with the Platonic Academy in Athens, which was headed at the time by Longinus, but Longinus was familiar with his work, partly at least through Porphyry who had studied in Athens. The fact that it was Rome where Plotinus set up his school may be due to the originality of his philosophical activity and to his patrons. He clearly had some influential contacts, not least with the philhellenic emperor Gallienus (253–268), who may also have encouraged his later failed attempt to set up a civic community based on Platonic principles in a ruined city in Campania.

Plotinus' school was, like most ancient schools of philosophy, relatively small in scale, but did attract distinguished students from abroad and from the Roman upper classes. It included not only philosophers but politicians and members of the medical profession who wished to lead the philosophical life. His most famous student was Porphyry (233–305 CE) who as a relative latecomer to the school persuaded him to put into writing the results of his seminars. It is almost certain that we possess most, if not all, of his written output, which represents his mature thought, since he didn't commence writing until the age of forty-eight. The school seemingly had inner and outer circles, and Plotinus himself was clearly an inspiring and sympathetic teacher who took a deep interest in the philosophical and spiritual progress of his students. Porphyry tells us that when he was suffering from severe depression Plotinus straight away visited him in his lodgings to help him. His concern for others is also illustrated by the fact that he was entrusted with the personal education of many orphans and the care of their property and careers. The reconciliation of this worldly involvement with the encouragement to lead a life of contemplation is encapsulated in Porphyry's comment that "he was present to himself and others at the same time."

The *Enneads* of Plotinus is the edition of his treatises arranged by his pupil Porphyry who tried to put shape to the collection he had inherited by organizing it into six sets of nine treatises (hence the name *"Enneads"*) that led the reader through the levels of Plotinus' universe, from the physical world to Soul, Intellect and, finally, to the highest principle, the One. Although Plotinus undoubtedly had a clearly structured metaphysical system by the time he began committing himself to expressing his thought in written form, the treatises themselves are not systematic expositions, but rather explorations of particular themes and issues raised in interpreting Plato and other philosophical texts read in the School. In fact, to achieve his neat arrangement Porphyry was sometimes driven even to dividing certain treatises (e.g., II.2–3; IV.3–5 and VI.4–5).

Although Plotinus' writings are not transcripts of his seminars, but are directed to the reader, they do, nevertheless, convey the sort of lively debate that he encouraged in his school. Frequently he takes for granted that a particular set of ideas is already familiar as having been treated in an earlier seminar that may or may not be found in the written text. For this reason it is useful for the reader to have some idea of the main philosophical principles of his system as they can be extracted from the *Enneads* as a whole.

Plotinus regarded himself as a faithful interpreter of Plato whose thought lies at the core of his entire project. But Plato's thought, whilst definitive, does according to Plotinus require careful exposition and clarification, often in the light of other thinkers such as Aristotle and the Stoics. It is because of this creative application of different traditions of ancient thought to the interpretation of Plato that Plotinus' version of Platonism became, partly through the medium of later Platonists such as Porphyry, Iamblichus (245–325) and Proclus (412–485), an influential source and way of reading both Plato and Aristotle in the Middle Ages, the Renaissance, and up to the mid 18th century, when scholars first began to differentiate Plato and "Neoplatonism." His thought, too, provided early Christian theologians of the Latin and particularly of the Byzantine tradition, with a rich variety of metaphysical concepts with which to explore and express difficult doctrinal ideas. His fashioning of Plato's ideas into a consistent metaphysical structure, though no longer accepted as a uniquely valid way of approaching Plato, was influential in promoting the notion of metaphysical systems in early modern philosophy. More recently increasing interest has centered on his exploration of the self, levels of consciousness, and his expansion of discourse beyond the levels of normal ontology to the examination of what lies both above and beneath being. His thought continues to challenge us when confronted with the issue of man's nature and role in the universe and of the extent and limitations of human knowledge.

Whilst much of Plotinus' metaphysical structure is recognizably an interpretation of Plato it is an interpretation that is not always immediately obvious just because it is filtered through several centuries of developing Platonic thought, itself already overlaid with important concepts drawn from other schools. It is, nevertheless, useful as a starting point to see how Plotinus attempts to bring coherence to what he believed to be a comprehensive worldview expressed in the Platonic dialogues. The Platonic Forms are central. They become for him an intelligible universe that is the source and model of the physical universe. But aware of Aristotle's criticism of the Platonic Forms as lifeless causes he takes on board Aristotle's concept of god as a self-thinker to enable him to identify this intelligible universe as a divine Intellect that thinks itself as the Forms or Intelligibles. The doctrine of the Forms as the thoughts of God had already entered Platonism, but not as the rigorously argued identity that Plotinus proposed. Moreover the Intelligibles, since they are identical with Intellect, are themselves actively intellectual; they are intellects. Thus Plato's world of Forms has become a complex and dynamic intelligible universe in which unity and plurality, stability and activity are reconciled.

Now although the divine Intellect is one it also embraces plurality both because its thoughts, the Intelligibles, are many and because it may itself be analyzed into thinker and thought. Its unity demands a further principle which is the cause of its unity. This principle which is the cause of all unity and being, but does not possess unity or being in itself, he calls the One, an interpretation of the Idea of the Good in Plato's *Republic* that is "beyond being" and that may be seen as the simple (hence "one") source of all reality. We thus have the first two of what subsequently became known as the three Hypostases, the One, Intellect, and Soul, the last of which acts as an intermediary between the intelligible and physical universes. This last Hypostasis takes on all the functions of transmitting form and life that may be found in Plato, although Plato himself does not always make such a clear distinction between soul and intellect. Thus the One is the ultimate source of all, including this universe, which is then prefigured in Intellect and transmitted through Soul to become manifest as our physical universe. Matter, which receives imperfectly this expression, is conceived not as an independently existing counter-principle, a dangerously dualist notion, but is in a sense itself a product of the One, a kind of non-being that, while being nothing specific in itself, nevertheless is not simply not there.

But this procession from an ultimate principle is balanced by a return movement at each level of reality that fully constitutes itself only when it turns back in contemplation of its producer. And so the whole of reality is a dynamic movement of procession and return, except for matter, which has no life of its own to make this return; it is inert. This movement of return, which may be traced back to the force of "love" in Plato or Aristotle's final cause, is characterized by Plotinus as a cognitive activity, a form of contemplation, weaker at each successive level, from Intellect through discursive reasoning to the merest image of rational order as expressed in the objects of the physical universe.

The human individual mirrors this structure to which we are all related at each level. For each of us has a body and soul, an intellect, and even something within us that relates to the One. While it is the nature of soul to give life to body, the higher aspect of our soul also has aspirations towards intellect, the true self, and even beyond. This urge to return corresponds to the cosmic movement of return.

But the tension between soul's natural duty to body and its origins in the intelligible can be, for the individual, a source of fracture and alienation in which the soul becomes over-involved and overwhelmed by the body and so estranged from its true self. Plotinus encourages us to make the return or ascent, but at the same time attempts to resolve the conflict of duties by reconciling the two-fold nature of soul as life-giving and contemplative.

This is the general framework within which important traditional philosophical issues are encountered, discussed and resolved, but always in a spirit of inquiry and ongoing debate. Issues are frequently encountered in several different contexts, each angle providing a different insight. The nature of the soul and its relationship to the body is examined at length (IV) using the Aristotelian distinctions of levels of soul (vegetative, growth, sensitive, rational) whilst maintaining the immortal nature of the transcendent soul in Platonic terms. The active nature of the soul in sense-perception is maintained to preserve the principle that incorporeals cannot be affected by corporeal reality. A vigorous discussion (VI.4 and 5) on the general nature of the relationship of incorporeals to body explores in every detail and in great depth the way in which incorporeals act on body. A universe that is the product of design is reconciled with the freedom of the individual. And, not least, the time-bound nature of the physical universe and human reason is grounded in the life of Intellect which subsists in eternity. Sometimes, however, Plotinus seems to break outside the framework of traditional metaphysics: the nature of matter and the One, each as non-being, though in a different sense, strains the terminology and structure of traditional ontology; and the attempt to reconcile the role of the individual soul within the traditional Platonic distinction of transcendent and immanent reality leads to a novel exploration of the nature of the self, the "I."

It is this restless urge for exploration and inquiry that lends to the treatises of Plotinus their philosophical vitality. Whilst presenting us with a rich and complexly coherent system, he constantly engages us in philosophical inquiry. In this way each treatise presents us with new ideas and fresh challenges. And, for Plotinus, every philosophical engagement is not just a mental exercise but also contributes to the rediscovery of the self and our reintegration with the source of all being, the Platonic aim of "becoming like god."

While Plotinus, like Plato, always wishes to engage his audience to reflect for themselves, his treatises are not easy reading, partly no doubt because his own audience was already familiar with many of his basic ideas and, more importantly, had been exposed in his seminars to critical readings of philosophical texts that have not survived to our day. Another problem is that the treatises do not lay out his thought in a systematic way but take up specific issues, although always the whole system may be discerned in the background. Sometimes, too, the exact flow of thought is difficult to follow because of an often condensed mode of expression. Because we are convinced that Plotinus has something to say to us today we have launched this series of translations and commentaries as a means of opening up the text to readers with an interest in grappling with the philosophical issues revealed by an encounter with Plotinus' own words and arguments. Each volume will contain a new translation, careful summaries of the arguments and structure of the treatise, and a philosophical commentary that will aim to throw light on the philosophical meaning and import of the text.

John M. Dillon
Andrew Smith

Abbreviations

DK *Die Fragmente der Vorsokratiker,* 6th ed. Revised by W. Kranz. Berlin: 1952.

HS_1 *Plotini Opera* I–III (editio maior), edited by P. Henry and H.-R. Schwyzer. Bruxelles: 1951–1973.

HS_2 *Plotini Opera* I–III (editio minor, with revised text), edited by P. Henry and H.-R. Schwyzer. Oxford: 1964–1982. When HS_1 HS_2 agree, HS indicates this.

LSJ *A Greek-English Lexicon.* H. Liddell & R. Scott, 9th ed. Revised by H. Jones. Oxford: 1940.

SVF *Stoicorum Veterum Fragmenta*, edited by H. von Arnim. Leipzig: 1905–1924.

VP *Vita Plotini* = Porphyry's Life of Plotinus printed at start of HS_1, HS_2, MacKenna and Armstrong.

Acknowledgments

THE AUTHOR WOULD LIKE TO THANK the editors, John Dillon and Andrew Smith, for their invitation to prepare this volume and for their advice and encouragement. I have also had the benefit of discussions regarding the translation and interpretation of Plotinus with George Boys-Stones, Richard King, and James Wilberding. All these scholars have been my collaborators in an ongoing engagement with one of the great philosophers of antiquity. I am also grateful to Eliza Tutellier, Sara Hermann, and Gale Carr for their enthusiastic support of this project.

Introduction to the Treatise

THE TREATISE LISTED BY PORPHYRY as number 32, and placed fifth in the fifth *Ennead*, bears the title "That the Intelligibles are not External to the Intellect, and on the Good." It is almost certainly a continuation of the treatise listed as 31, but placed eighth in the fifth *Ennead*, titled "On the Intelligible Beauty." This is the universal conclusion of scholars based on two considerations. First is the fact that the first line of V.5 seems to respond to the question that ends V.8: "Is what has been said sufficient to lead us to clarity regarding the intelligible region, or should we go back again and take another path like this . . .?" The first two chapters of V.5 appear to pursue this alternate path. Second, and somewhat looser, is the consideration that V.8 aims to lead the reader to ascend to Intellect in order to contemplate the One (see V.8 [31] 1, 1–7). In V.5 [32], beginning in chapter 3, the rest of the treatise is devoted to a discussion of the One, and especially Intellect's relation to it. A more contentious claim, elaborated on by Harder (see Commentary below on 4, 1–6, p. 119) is that treatises 31 and 32 are themselves the central parts of a larger treatise comprised of III.8 [30], V.8 [31], V.5 [32], and II.9 [33]. Since there is no reason to doubt the chronological ordering of the treatises given by Porphyry, not much turns on whether III.8 was written shortly before the others and II.9 shortly after the others, or whether in some sense they were intended to be read together as one treatise.

This treatise divides, then, into two unequal parts, sections 1–2 and 3–13. The first section is focused on a problem derived from the correct interpretation of a passage in Plato's *Timaeus*. At 39e6–9, in describing the work of the Demiurge in importing intelligibility into the pre-cosmic chaos, Timaeus says, "This remaining task he accomplished, fashioning the world according to the nature of the paradigm. And so he determined that this world should contain the same kind and number of things that intellect sees are contained in the Living Animal." The problem is that it is difficult to know whether Plato means that the Living Animal and all that it contains exists external to the intellect that the Demiurge is or whether the Living Animal is somehow or other identical with that intellect. The former possibility is suggested by the fact that the Demiurge "looks" (*kathorai*) at intelligibles; the latter is suggested by a comparison of the present passage with 29e3 and 30d2 where the Demiurge wants the world both to be made the same as the Living Animal and as near as possible like himself. These two passages taken together suggest that if the world is made the same as the Living Animal it thereby is made the same as the Demiurge himself because the contents of the Living Animal are internal to the intellect that the Demiurge is.

Platonists beginning in the Old Academy itself and up to and including Plotinus struggled to provide argument for one or another of these alternatives. As we shall see in our treatise itself, the solution depends heavily on how Intellect and the Forms or intelligibles are to be understood in relation to the first principle of all, the One or the Good. Proclus (412–485) has an illuminating discussion of the possible solutions found among his predecessors in his *Commentary on Plato's* Timaeus (1.323, 22–324, 10). The solution that Plotinus proposes, namely, that the intelligibles are not external to the Intellect, is a fundamental building block in his systematic construction of Platonism. As will be discussed in the commentaries, the solution is intended to be consistent with the analysis showing the utter simplicity of the One and, therefore, the necessary complexity of everything else, including Intellect. Plotinus thereby shows that Aristotle's Unmoved Mover, which according to Aristotle must be absolutely simple if it is to be a first principle, cannot in fact be so. The solution also reflects the argument that cognition must be paradigmatically infallible, but that if the intelligibles are external to Intellect, it is at least possible that the Intellect, which must then somehow represent that which is external to it, can fail to represent intelligibles correctly. That infallible cognition must be instantiated will be the conclusion of two arguments: (1) that if there is no infallible cognition, truth will not exist, and (2) if infallible cognition does not exist, our embodied higher cognition could not be possible. The first argument is concerned with "ontological" truth, that is, the property of being that makes it intelligible to us and makes it possible for us to grasp the truth about the world in predicative judgments. The second argument leads Plotinus to another contentious conclusion, namely, that all human beings have undescended intellects which are (infallibly) cognizing all intelligibles right now.

The second part of this treatise focuses on the One and Intellect's relation to it. Just as Intellect is necessarily infallibly cognizing all intelligibles and thereby explaining the intelligibility of its images, so the One is necessary to account for the being of Intellect and the intelligibles internal to it. The absolute simplicity of the One follows from its unique explanatory primacy. Among other things, this means that the One is "above *ousia*" as Plato says of the Good in *Republic* 509b8. If the One *did* possess an *ousia* of any sort, then it would be irreducibly complex, that is, there would be a distinction between it or its existence and its *ousia*. This is the conclusion Plotinus draws from the deduction at *Parmenides* 142b5–8 regarding a one which is. Because the One is above *ousia*, it is not limited in any way. That is, it does not possess the limitation that follows from being one kind of thing rather than another. Because it is unlimited, there is nowhere it is not nor is there anything which does not participate in it in some way. The ubiquity of the One is the principal reason for our lack of awareness of its existence.

Since the overall theme of the combined treatise V.8 and V.5 is the ascent to the One or Good via Intellect, Plotinus addresses in section 12 the relation between beauty and the Good, for beauty is the relational "property" of the Good as attractive to us. The Good itself is prior to beauty, which here as elsewhere is identified with all the Forms (see I.6 [1] 9, 15 and V.8 [31] 9, 40–42). That which draws us to the Good is precisely form, which appeals to us first as sensible and then, as the aspirant progresses in philosophy, purely as intelligible. Following Plato and Aristotle, Plotinus maintains that the real Good is what all desire, though human beings are content with apparent beauty. This does not mean that apparent beauty is really something else; it means that the Good, which is the source of all beauty and hence, what beauty is virtually, only appears as beautiful to us. The difference between the philosopher and everyone else, according to Plotinus, is that the former recognizes that the apparently beautiful is not in fact the Good, whereas the latter do not.

For the text of V.5, I have used the *editio minor* of *Plotini Opera* by Paul Henry and Hans-Rudolph Schwyzer, vol. 2 (Oxford, 1977). I have also consulted the *Addenda ad Textum* contained in vol. 3 (Oxford, 1983). The English translation of the *Enneads* by Stephen MacKenna, originally published in five volumes (London, 1917–1930) and most conveniently available in a second edition in one volume, revised by B. S. Page (London, 1956), is a magnificent achievement and still eminently worth consulting, although the translation is not adequate for scholarly use since it is not based on the later critical edition by Henry and Schwyzer. I have continually consulted the equally splendid work of A. H. Armstrong, a translation of the *Enneads* in 7 volumes (Cambridge, MA, 1966–1988). The French translation and commentary by Richard Dufour (2006) in the 9 volume set of translations of and commentaries on all the *Enneads*, edited by Luc Brisson and Jean-François Pradeau (Paris, 2002–2010), has been extremely helpful.

Note on the Text

LINE NUMBERS IN THE TRANSLATION are approximate and do not always match the original Greek text. Since the commentary follows the sequence of the English translation, there may sometimes be a slight discrepancy in the ordering.

The Greek text adopted is that of the Oxford edition (taking into account the *Addenda ad Textum* in vol. 3, 304–325). Deviations from the text are noted in the commentary. Each *Ennead* is referred to by Roman numerals, followed by the number of the treatise, the chapter of the treatise, and, finally, separated by a comma, the line number or numbers, e.g, V.1.3, 24–27.

It is customary to add the chronological number given by Porphyry in his *Life of Plotinus (Vita Plotini),* so that, for example, V.1. is designated V.1 [10]. In this series the chronological number is given only where it is of significance for Plotinus' philosophical stance. The following charts indicate the chronological order.

It should be noted that Plotinus did not provide titles to the treatises and that these were later added by Porphyry when preparing his edition from those that had become traditional amongst the readers of Plotinus' manuscripts (see Porphyrpy *VP* 4), although Porphyry himself sometimes gives different titles to the same treatise in his chronological *VP* 4–6) and thematic (*VP* 24–25) lists, and variant titles are also found in Simplicius and Philoponus in the 6th century.

Chronological Order of the *Enneads*

Enn.		*Enn.*		*Enn.*		*Enn.*		*Enn.*		*Enn.*	
I.1	**53**	II.1	**40**	III.1	**3**	IV.1	**21**	V.1	**10**	VI.1	**42**
I.2	**19**	II.2	**14**	III.2	**47**	IV.2	**4**	V.2	**11**	VI.2	**43**
I.3	**20**	II.3	**52**	III.3	**48**	IV.3	**27**	V.3	**49**	VI.3	**44**
I.4	**46**	II.4	**12**	III.4	**15**	IV.4	**28**	V.4	**7**	VI.4	**22**
I.5	**36**	II.5	**25**	III.5	**50**	IV.5	**29**	V.5	**32**	VI.5	**23**
I.6	**1**	II.6	**17**	III.6	**26**	IV.6	**41**	V.6	**24**	VI.6	**34**
I.7	**54**	II.7	**37**	III.7	**45**	IV.7	**2**	V.7	**18**	VI.7	**38**
I.8	**51**	II.8	**35**	III.8	**30**	IV.8	**6**	V.8	**31**	VI.8	**39**
I.9	**16**	II.9	**33**	III.9	**13**	IV.9	**8**	V.9	**5**	VI.9	**9**

	Enn.		*Enn.*		*Enn.*		*Enn.*		*Enn.*		*Enn.*
1	I.6	**10**	V.1	**19**	I.2	**28**	IV.4	**37**	II.7	**46**	I.4
2	IV.7	**11**	V.2	**20**	I.3	**29**	IV.5	**38**	VI.7	**47**	III.2
3	III.1	**12**	II.4	**21**	IV.1	**30**	III.8	**39**	VI.8	**48**	III.3
4	IV.2	**13**	III.9	**22**	VI.4	**31**	V.8	**40**	II.1	**49**	V.3
5	V.9	**14**	II.2	**23**	VI.5	**32**	V.5	**41**	IV.6	**50**	III.5
6	IV.8	**15**	III.4	**24**	V.6	**33**	II.9	**42**	VI.1	**51**	I.8
7	V.4	**16**	I.9	**25**	II.5	**34**	VI.6	**43**	VI.2	**52**	II.3
8	IV.9	**17**	II.6	**26**	III.6	**35**	II.8	**44**	VI.3	**53**	I.1
9	VI.9	**18**	V.7	**27**	IV.3	**36**	I.5	**45**	III.7	**54**	I.7

Synopsis

Chapter 1 — Truth must be internal to Intellect

1–32 If intelligibles were not internal to Intellect, Intellect's cognition could be fallible.

32–50 Intelligibles themselves have life and intellect and are not separable from each other.

50–68 If intelligibles are external to Intellect, Intellect does not possess truth and it is deceived if it supposes that it does. It will have only representations of the truth.

Chapter 2

Intellect, therefore, is cognitively identified with all intelligibles, thereby possessing the truth, ontologically speaking.

1–12 How Intellect is identified with intelligibles.

12–24 Intellect's cognition of intelligibles is immediate and non-inferential. Intellect is not subject to refutation.

Chapter 3 — Intellect is "second god" coming from the first god

1–4 The second god is the locus of all being.

4–24 The first principle of all is the first god and reigns supreme over everything.

Chapter 4 — On the relation been the One and numbers

1–6 The unity of Intellect is inferior to the absolute One.

6–16 The sense in which the One is absolutely or unqualifiedly one.

16–38 The One is not an essential number or Number Form; nor is it the principle of number. It is not an element of the Indefinite Dyad.

Chapter 5 — The One is that which produces everything. It produces intelligible being first

1–14 The One is not participated in as if it were a principle of number. The One, in producing everything, does not go out of itself.

14–28 The etymology of the word "being" (einai), derived from the word "one" (hen).

Chapter 6 — On the nature of the One

1–14 The One is without form and so it transcends being.

14–37 Attainment of the One that is unknowable. The need for negative theology.

Chapter 7 — The analogy of the Intellect to sight

1–21 Analogy of the activity of intellection to the activity of seeing.

21–35 Like the eye, Intellect possesses an interior illumination.

Chapter 8 — Strategies for attaining to the One

1–23 The omnipresence of the One as of light.

23–7 The One is everywhere and nowhere.

Chapter 9 — The "nesting" of Soul in Intellect and Intellect in the One

1–18 The lower is always in the higher.

18–26 The omnipresence of the One.

26–38 Everything is ultimately in the One, which is in nothing.

Chapter 10 — The One, being the cause of everything, is unlike all things

1–5 The One must be sought directly without intermediaries.

5–23 The One is unlimited in power and identical with the Good.

Chapter 11 — The reality of the immaterial first principle of all

1–5 The One is in every way unlimited.

5–22 People who think that the real is the material are deprived of divinity.

Chapter 12 — The Good is prior to the Beautiful

1–5 The necessity of approaching the One with thought alone.

5–19 The desire for the Good is prior to the desire for that which is beautiful.

19–40 The ways in which people confuse the Good with the beautiful.

40–50 The Good needs nothing and produces everything.

Chapter 13 — The absolute simplicity and transcendence of the Good

1–11 The Good possesses nothing. Adding anything to it subtracts from it.

11–20 It is necessary to remove all predicates from the Good.

20–32 The Good is not good by participating in or having goodness.

33–38 The superiority and absolute simplicity of the Good, the first principle of all.

Translation of Plotinus Ennead *V.5 [32]*

That the Intelligibles are not External to the Intellect, and on the Good

1. Might, then, one say that Intellect—the true and real Intellect—will ever be in error and have beliefs about the things that are not?[1] Not at all. For how would Intellect still be what it is if it is unthinking? It must, therefore, always know and not ever forget, and its knowledge | must not be conjecture, or uncertain, or like something heard at second hand. So, then, its knowledge is not acquired by means of demonstration either. For even if someone were to say that some of what it knows it knows by means of demonstration, in that case there would still be something self-evident to it. Actually, our argument maintains that

1 This treatise is continuous with V.8. The last sentence of that treatise is: "So, is what has been said sufficient to lead to a clear understanding of the intelligible realm, or should we go back and take another path like this one?"

everything is self-evident to it. For how could someone distinguish the things that are self-evident to it from those that are not?

But as for those things they concede are self-evident | to it—from where will they say their being self-evident comes?[2] And from where will Intellect derive the conviction that things are self-evident to it? For even sensibles, though they seem to bring with them the most self-evident conviction, do not, in fact, convince us that their apparent existence is in underlying subjects rather than in our experiences, | and that they are not in need of intellect or discursive reasoning to make judgments about them. For even if it is agreed that the sensibles are in their underlying subjects, the apprehension of which sense-perception will bring about, what is known by means of sense-perception of the object is a reflected representation of the thing; it is not the thing itself that sense-perception receives, for that object remains external.

| Given that when Intellect knows, it knows intelligibles, how, if these are different from it, would it connect with them? For it is possible that it does not, so that it is possible that it does not know, or knows them only at the time when it connected with them and will not always have the knowledge. But if they will say that they are linked to it, what does the term "linked" mean? In that case, acts of

---

2 I.e., Epicureans. See Sextus Empiricus, *Against the Professors* 8.9 and 7.203.

intellection will be impressions. | And if this is so, they act externally, that is, they are impacts. But how will these impressions be made, and what will be the shape of such things? And in that case, an act of intellection will be of externals just like sense-perception. And in what way will it differ from sense-perception other than by apprehending something smaller? And how will it know that it really apprehended them? And how will it know that something is good or beautiful or | just? For each of these will be other than the object, and the principles of judgment by which it will attain conviction will not be in it, but rather these will be external, and the truth will be there.

And then, either intelligibles are themselves without sense-perception and without any portion of life and intellect, or they do have intellect. And if they have intellect, both are simultaneously here—this truth and this primary Intellect—| and we shall investigate in addition what the truth here is like, and whether the intelligible and Intellect are identical and occur simultaneously, and yet are still two and different—or how are they related? But if the intelligibles are nonintelligent or without life, what sort of realities are they?[3] For they are not "premises" or "axioms" or "sayables"[4]; if they were, straightaway they

3 See Plato, *Sophist* 248e.

4 The premises are the supposedly self-evident propositional truths that form the basis of Aristotelian demonstrations. See *Prior Analytics*, 1.1.24a16–b15. The axioms and "sayables" are Stoic. See *SVF* 2.132, 149, 153, 166, 168, 169.

would be referring to things different from themselves, and | they would not then be the things themselves. For example, if they will say "that which is just is beautiful," that which is just and that which is beautiful are in fact other than what is said. But if they say that these are "simples," justice being separate from beauty, then, first, the intelligible realm will not be some one thing nor in one thing, but each intelligible will be dispersed. And where and in what places will they be dispersed? And how will Intellect hit upon them, | meandering through these places? How will it remain undisturbed—or rather, how will it remain in the identical place? In general, what sort of shape or impression will it have of them? Or are we to assume that they are like constructed golden images or some other matter produced by some sculptor or engraver? But if they are like this, the contemplating of Intellect will in fact be sense-perception. Further, why is one of these things | Justice and another something else?

But the greatest objection is this. If, indeed, one were to grant that these intelligibles are totally external to Intellect, and then claim that Intellect contemplates them as such, it necessarily follows that it does not itself have the truth of these things and that it is deceived in all that it contemplates: for it is those intelligibles that would be the true reality. It will contemplate | them though it does not have them, instead receiving reflected representations of them in a kind of cognition like this. Then, not having true reality, but rather receiving for itself reflected representations of the truth, it will have falsities and nothing true. If, then, it knows that it has falsities, it will agree that it has no share in truth. But if it is ignorant of this as well, and | thinks that it has the truth when it does not, the falsity that is generated in it is double, and that will separate it considerably from the truth.

This is the reason, I think, that in acts of sense-perception, too, truth is not found, but only belief, because belief is receptive,[5] and for this reason, being belief, | it receives something other than that from which it receives what it has. If, then, there is no truth in Intellect, an intellect of this sort will not be truth nor will it be truly Intellect, nor will it be Intellect at all. But there is nowhere else for the truth to be.

2. One should not, then, seek for intelligibles external to Intellect, nor assert that there are impressions of real things in it, nor, depriving it of truth, make it ignorant of intelligibles and make them non-existent, and even eliminate Intellect itself. But since | one must bring in knowledge and truth, that is, preserve real beings and knowledge of what each of them is—but not of their qualities, inasmuch as in having these, we would have only a reflected representation and a trace of reality, and we would not have or

5 Taking the word for belief, *doxa*, from the word for "receive" *dechomai*.

be present with or mixed with the things themselves—all real beings should be given to true Intellect. For in this way it would know, that is, | truly know, and not forget, nor would it meander seeking them, and the truth will be in it, and it will be the foundation for these real beings, and they will be alive and will be thinking.

All of this must belong to the most blessed nature anyway; otherwise, where will its honor and dignity be? Indeed, again, this being the case, it will also have no need of demonstration or of conviction that these things are so— | because it is itself the way that it is and it is self-evident to itself that it is this way; and if there is something prior to it, that is because it is self-evident to it that it comes from that; and if something comes after what is prior to it, that is because it is self-evident to it that that is itself—and no one can be more convinced of this than it is—and because in the intelligible world it is this and really so. So, the real truth is also not its being in harmony with something else, but with itself, and it expresses nothing else beside itself, but | what it expresses, it is, and what it is, this is also what it expresses. Who, then, could refute it? And from where would one draw the refutation? For the refutation adduced would rely on the identical thing said before, and even if you were to provide something else, it is brought in line with that which was said originally and it is one with that. For you could not find anything truer than the truth.

3. There is, then, for us, one nature, which is Intellect, all real beings, and the truth. And if this is so, it is a great god; rather, it is not *a* god, but one might well think that that which is all real beings is the universal god. And this nature is god, a second god, revealing itself before we see the first. That first god | is seated or settled above Intellect, as if on a sort of beautiful pedestal which is suspended from it. For it had to be the case that the One, in proceeding, did not proceed to something soulless, nor, indeed, even proceed immediately to Soul, but that there had to be an indescribable beauty leading its way,[6] just as in the procession of a great king, the | lesser come first, and the greater and more dignified come after them in turn, and those who are even closer to the king are more regal, and those after them even more honored. After all these, the Great King suddenly reveals himself, with the people praying to him and prostrating themselves, at least those who have not already left, thinking that it was enough | to see those who preceded the king.

So this king is other than those who proceed before him, who are other than him. But in the intelligible world, the king is not a foreign ruler; rather, he has the most just rule by nature, and true kingship, since he is the king of truth, and by nature sovereign | of the massed ranks of his own offspring, a divine battalion; is king of the king

6 See Plato, *Republic* 509a6.

and of kings, and would more justly be called father of gods than Zeus.[7] Zeus imitated him in this, not holding himself to the contemplation of his father, but imitating what is in a way the activity of his grandfather which is realized in the existence of essence.

4. It has been said, then, that it is necessary to make the ascent to a one, that is, to what is truly one, but not in the way that other things are one, which, being many, are one by partaking of a one—we must grasp that which is not one by participation, not that which is not more one than it is many—and it has also been said that the intelligible universe, that is, | Intellect, is more one than anything else, and that there is nothing that is nearer the One itself, though it is not purely one.

Now we long to see that which is purely and really one and not one owing to something else, if this is in some way possible. It is necessary, then, to rush towards the One from here, and not to add anything else to it, but to stop in absolute fear of | separating ourselves from it; and not to proceed to duality in the least bit. If you don't do this, you get two, among which the One is not; rather, both will be posterior to it. For it does not wish to be counted with something different from it no matter whether that is one or how many; indeed, it does not wish to be numbered at

7 See Homer, *Iliad* 1.544.

all. For it is a measure and is not measured, and it is not equal to other things, such that that it is among them. | If this were not the case, there will be something common to it and the things numbered, and that would be prior to it. But there cannot be anything prior to it.

Not even the term "essential number" applies to it, let alone what is posterior to this, namely, "quantitative number." For essential number is that which eternally provides being, whereas quantitative number provides quantity with other things or even without other things, | since this is a number.[8] Since the nature of quantitative numbers is produced as an imitation in relation to the one which is their principle (that being among the prior numbers, which are themselves imitations in relation to the true One), it does not exist by using up or fragmenting its unity, which is a monad prior to a duality that comes from it. And this monad is | not each of the ones in the duality nor is it one of them while not being the other. For why would it be one rather than another? If, then, it is neither of them, it is other and, though it remains what it is, it does not remain isolated.

How, then, are the ones in the duality different from each other? And how is the duality one? Is the one of the duality identical to the one in each part of the duality? In fact, we have to say that they participate in the primary

8 See below 5, 11–13.

one, being other than that in which | they participate, and the duality, insofar as it is one, also participates, but not in the same way, just as an army and a house are not one in the same way. A house is one insofar as it is continuous; it is not essentially one, nor is it a one in quantity.

So, are the monads in the pentad other than the monads in the decad, while the one that unifies the pentad is identical to the one that unifies the | decad? In fact, if every ship is compared with every other ship, small and large, and every city with every other, and every army with every other, the one in them is identical in each case. But if it is not in these cases, then neither is it for those. If, then, there are certain puzzles remaining regarding these matters, we will take them up later.[9]

5. But we should return to the point where it was said that the First remains identical even if other things should come from it. In the case of numbers, then, the one remains while another one produces, and the number is generated according to that one. But in that which precedes real beings, here the One | remains by itself much more. And though it remains, it is not the case that another does the producing, if real beings are produced by it; rather, it is sufficient itself for generating real beings. And just as there in the case of quantitative numbers, there was a first—the

---

9 See *Ennead* VI.6: *On Number.*

monad— which was a form primarily and secondarily for all of them, that is, the individual numbers which | came after it do not participate equally in it, so in the case of essential numbers, each of the things that came after the First has within itself something of it as a sort of form. And for quantitative numbers, participation brought into existence the quantity of the numbers, whereas for essential numbers participation brought into existence their essence, so that their being is a trace of the One.

And if someone says that the word "being" (*einai*)—the name that | indicates essence—comes from "one" (*hen*), he may have hit on the truth. For that which is said to "be" first proceeded a little from the One, in a way, and did not wish to go still further, but turned within itself and stood there (*estē*), and became essence, the "hearth" (*hestia*) of all things. It is as if | someone who utters the sound ("*einai*"), starting with the sound (*hen*), reveals that which is from the One, and signifies being (*on*), insofar as possible. Thus, that which come to be, essence and being, have an imitation that flows from the power of the One. And essence looking at and being moved by the sight, imitating what it saw, let out the | sound "is" (*on*) and "being" (*einai*) and "essence" (*ousia*) and "hearth" (*hestia*). Thus, the sounds want to indicate the being of the one who, in pain, gave birth to the sounds. They imitate, so far as is possible, the generation of real being.

6. But let these remarks be taken as one wishes. An essence that is generated is a form—for someone could not say that what is generated from there is anything else. And it is not a form of something, but of everything. So, the One is necessarily | without form. And being without form, it is not essence. For the essence must be a "this something," and this is defined. But it is not possible to grasp the One as a "this." For it would at once no longer be a principle, but only that thing which you said was a "this."

But if all things are found within that which is generated, which among these will you say that the One is? Since it is no one of these, it can only | be said to be beyond them. These are real things, that is, being. Therefore, it is beyond being. For "that which is beyond being" does not indicate a "this"—it does not posit it as such—nor does it indicate its name, but implies only that it is not this. If this is what the expression does, it does not at all *encompass* the One. For it would be absurd to seek to encompass this | unlimited nature. Someone who wanted to do this would have immediately prevented himself from in any way advancing toward a trace of the One. But just as someone who wants to see the intelligible nature, will, if he has no image of the sensible nature, be able to contemplate that which is beyond the sensible, so someone | wishing to contemplate that which is beyond the intelligible will contemplate it by setting aside all that is intelligible, because while he learns that it is by means of the intelligible, he learns the way in which it is by setting the intelligible aside. "The way it is" might as well be "the way it is not," for the "way it is" is not in anything or a "something." But we in our birth pains to say something are necessarily at a loss, and we are speaking about that which is inexpressible, | and wishing to give it a name, we are trying insofar as we are able to make it clear to ourselves.

But perhaps the name "One" contains an elimination of plurality. It is owing to this as well that the Pythagoreans symbolically meant the One when among themselves they referred to "Apollo" as the negation of plurality (*a-pollōn*). And if the One is affirmed both as the name and as that which the name indicates, this | would be less clear than if someone did not say that name. For perhaps this name was used so that someone who started their inquiry from that which indicates what is absolutely simple would end up negating this, too. For though it was asserted as well as could be by the one who asserts it, this has no value for clarifying its nature, | because that cannot be heard nor can it be understood by one who hears, but by one who sees, if by anyone at all. But if the one who is seeing seeks to look at a form, he will not see the One.

7. So, again, since the activity of seeing is twofold, as with the eye—one is the thing seen by it, the form of the sensible, the other is that light by means of which it sees the form, and this itself is sensible, and though it is

different from | the form, and the cause of the seeing of it, it is seen in the form, that is, along with it. For this reason, the light does not at that moment provide a clear sense-perception of itself inasmuch as the eye is directed to that which has been illuminated. But when there is nothing else but it, the eye sees it in an instant impression, though even then the eye sees it being supported by something else, since if | it came into being alone, and not in relation to something other, sense-perception would not be able to grasp it. For even the light of the sun, the light which is in it, would perhaps escape sense-perception if it were deprived of the mass that supported it. But if someone were to say that the sun is all light, one could take this as a clarification of what has been said. For light will be in none of the forms belonging to the | other things which are seen, and perhaps it will by itself be visible. For the other visible things are not light alone.

The vision of Intellect is, then, like this. It itself also sees by means of another light the things that are illuminated by that primary nature, and sees since the light is in them. But insofar as it inclines towards the nature of that which is illuminated, it sees it less. If it were to | set aside the things seen and were to look at that by means of which it sees, it would be looking at light and the source of light. But since it is necessary for Intellect to look at this light as not being external to it, we must go back to the eye. This at times will itself see not an external or alien light, but for a moment, something akin to it, prior to the external, and | more brilliant. Either it springs from the eye in the darkness of night or, when it does not want to look at other things, it lowers the eyelids and nevertheless emits light, or when the eyelids are shut, one sees the light in the eye. For then it sees without seeing and it is most of all | then that it sees. For then it sees light. And the other things it saw were light-like in their form, though they were not light.

In this way, Intellect, covering its eyes so that it does not see other things, and collecting itself into its interior, and not looking at anything, will see a light that is not other than it or in another, but itself by itself alone and pure, and it appears to it all of a sudden so that it is in doubt as to where it appeared from, externally or internally, | and when it goes away it says, "so it was internal—but, again, not internal."

8. In fact, one should not seek where it comes from. For there is not any "where"; it neither comes from nor goes anywhere, it both appears and does not appear. For this reason, it is necessary not to pursue it, but to remain in a tranquil state, until it should appear, preparing oneself to be a contemplator, just like the eye | awaits the rising sun. The sun rising over the horizon—the poets say "from Ocean"[10]—gives itself to be seen with the eyes.

10 Homer, *Iliad* 7.422.

But from where will that which the sun imitates arise? And rising over what horizon will it appear? In fact, it arises over the Intellect which contemplates it. For Intellect will be immobilized | in its contemplation, since it is looking at nothing else beside that which is beautiful, inclining and giving itself over completely to what is in the intelligible world; immobile and in a way filled with strength, it sees first itself becoming more beautiful, and shining, as it is near it. It did not, however, come as one expected; rather, it came as if it had not come. | For it was seen not as something coming, but as something present prior to everything, before Intellect came to it.

It is Intellect that comes and Intellect that goes away, because it does not know where it should wait and where the One is waiting, which is nowhere. And if it were possible for Intellect itself to wait nowhere—not in the sense that it is in place, for it is | not in place, but in the sense that it is altogether nowhere—it would be always looking at the One. And yet it would not be looking, but would be one with it, and not two. Now, however, because it is Intellect, when it looks, it looks in this way, by that in itself which is not Intellect. It is wondrous how it is present not because it has come, and how, not being anywhere, there is nowhere that it is not. It is, | then, immediately marveled at, but for one who knows, it would be marvelous if it were the opposite. Or rather: the opposite is not possible such that one could marvel at it. And this is how it is:

9. Everything that comes to be by something else is either in that which has made it or in something else, supposing there were to be something after that which made it. For since that which comes to be by another was also in need of that other for its generation, it needs that other everywhere, for which reason it is in another. So, things which are | by nature last in order are in the last things prior to them, which are in the things prior to them, and so on until one arrives at the principle which is first. But since the principle has nothing prior to itself, there is not any other in which it is. And not being in any other, it encompasses | all the other things which are in the things prior to themselves. Encompassing them, it is not scattered among them and it holds them and is not held by them. In holding them and in not being held by them, there is nowhere it is not. For if there is somewhere it is not, it does not hold what is there. But if something is not held, it is not there. So, it is present and not present by not being encompassed, and by being free of everything that | would prevent it from being anywhere. For, again, if it is prevented, it is limited by another, and things immediately after would have no share in it, and the god would only go this far, and would no longer be in control, but would be subservient to things after it.

The things which are in something, then, are there where that thing is. But as for things which are not somewhere, there is nowhere they are not. For if a thing is not *here*, it is clear that another place | contains it, and it is "here" somewhere else, making it false that it is nowhere. If, then, it is true that it is not anywhere and false that it is somewhere (without thereby implying that it is somewhere else), it is not separate from anything. And if it is not separate from anything, being nowhere, it will be everywhere self-contained. For there is not some part of it here, and some part there; nor is it even in one place as a whole. So, it is a | whole everywhere, with nothing holding it and nothing not holding it. Therefore, everything is held by it.

Consider the cosmos, too, which, since there is no cosmos prior to it, is not in a cosmos nor, again, in place. For what place could exist before the cosmos? Its parts are dependent on it and are in it. And Soul is not in the universe, | but rather the universe is in Soul. For the body is not a place in which Soul is, but Soul is in Intellect, body is in Soul, and Intellect in something else [the One]. And there is nothing else beyond this such that it would be in that. Therefore, it is in nothing at all. In this way, then, it is nowhere. Where, then, are other things? They are in it. Therefore, it is not cut off from other things nor is it in them | nor is there something holding it, but rather it holds everything. For this reason, and in this way, it is the Good of everything, because everything depends on it, each in a different way. For this reason, some things are better than others, because some things have more being than others.

10. But please do not, for my sake, look at it through other things. If you do that, you will see a trace of it, not it. But think what it would be to grasp that which is in itself, pure, mixed with nothing, all things partaking in it, but nothing holding it. For there is | nothing else of this sort, yet there must exist something of this sort. Who, then, could grasp its power as a whole? For if it is everything at once, how could something differ from it?

Does one, then, grasp it in part? But you who are approaching it, approach it comprehensively, even though you are not able to describe it as a whole. Otherwise, you will be an intellect thinking, and even if you chance on it, it will escape you, or | rather you will escape it. But when you try to see it, look at the whole. And when you think it, whatever you might remember of it, think that it is the Good—being virtually everything, it is the cause of intelligent life and thought, that from which comes life and intellect and whatever there is of essence and being—that it is one—for it is simple and first—that it is a principle—for from it | all things come.[11] The first motion is from it, for it is not in it, and from it is rest, because it did not need it, for "it does not move nor rest,"[12] for it has neither that in which it can rest nor that in which it can move.[13] For

11 See Plato, *Republic* 511b7.

12 See Plato, *Parmenides* 139b3.

13 See Plato, *Sophist* 254d5; *Parmenides* 138d4–5, 139a3–4.

around what or in relation to what or in what would it do these things? For it is first.

But it has not been limited.[14] For by what would it be so? | And yet it is not in magnitude that it is unlimited. For where would it have had to proceed to? Or in order to become what, given that it has no need of anything? No, it is insofar as it is power that it possesses unlimitedness, for it will never be otherwise nor will it lack anything, whereas it is because of it that there are things which are not lacking as well.

11. Further, this is unlimited by being not more than one, and it has nothing in relation to which something that comes from it will have a limit. For by being one it could not be measured nor will it amount to a number. It is not limited, then, in relation to something else or in relation to itself for in that case it would be two. Nor does it, then, have a figure, | because it has no parts, nor does it have a shape.

Do not seek this with mortal eyes, as our account says, nor seek to see it as would someone who thought that all things are sensible. By supposing that, he would eliminate what exists most of all. For those things which someone thinks to be most of all, are most of all not. And that which someone thinks | has great being has in fact less

14 See Plato, *Parmenides* 137d7–8.

of it. That which is first is the principle of being and even more properly first than essence. So, you should reverse your belief. If you don't, you will be left alone, bereft of god, like those at festivals stuffing themselves with food[15] (something that it is not lawful for those approaching the gods to do), believing that the food is | more substantial than the sight of the god (whom they should be celebrating), and not partaking of the rites within. For in these rites, the god, who is not seen, produces disbelief in those who only believe in things they can see clearly, which they only see with their flesh. It is as if there were people who slept throughout their lives and believed that their dreams were trustworthy and clear: if someone were to waken them, they would disbelieve what they saw with their own eyes, and they would go back to sleep.

12. It is necessary to look at each thing by that by which each should properly be perceived; some things are perceived with the eyes, others with the ears, and others by other means. And one should trust that other things are seen with the intellect, and not believe that thinking is done by hearing or seeing, just as if someone were to command one to see with the ears, and to claim that there were no | sounds because they were not seen. It is also necessary to consider how people have forgotten what they originally

15 See Plato, *Phaedo* 81e5.

desired, and even now long for and desire. For all things desire and pursue that by a necessity of nature, as if they had divined that without which they are not able to exist.

And the apprehension of that which is beautiful is there already for those who in a way know it and | have wakened to it, and so, too, the amazement, the awakening of love. But the Good, since it was present of old to an innate desire, and is also present to those who are asleep, does not amaze those who sometimes see it, because it is always with them and there is never a recollection of it. People do not see it because it is present when they are asleep. But the love of that which is beautiful, when it is | present, gives pain, because one must desire it once having seen it. This love is secondary, and the fact that lovers are conscious of it at once reveals the beauty also to be secondary. But the desire that is more ancient than this, and imperceptible, declares the Good to be more ancient and prior.

Everyone thinks that, having gotten the Good, that is sufficient for them, | for they think that they have thereby arrived at their goal. But not all see that which is beautiful, and when it is generated, they think that it is beautiful in itself rather than beautiful for them, just in the way it is with beauty here, for it is the beauty of the one who has it. And for them, it is sufficient if things seem beautiful, even if they are not. This is not how they stand in regard to that which is good.[16] For they argue and compete and quarrel | especially about the primacy of beauty, since they think that beauty has come to be in the way they do. It is as if one who was last in the royal line wanted to attain the same position as the one who is first in line, on the grounds that they both have their origin in the king himself, ignoring the fact that, although he does derive his status from the king as well, | the other man comes before him.

The explanation for the error is that both participate in the identical thing, that is, the One, which is prior to both, and that in the intelligible world, the Good is not in need of that which is beautiful, whereas that which is beautiful needs it. The Good is gentle, pleasant, and most delicate, and present to someone just when they wish it. But that which is beautiful brings | amazement, shock and pain mixed with the pleasure. That which is beautiful even draws away from the Good those who do not know it, as a beloved draws one away from one's father, for that which is beautiful is younger. The Good is prior not in time, but in truth, which has a prior power. For it has all the power. That which comes after it does not have | all the power, but as much as there is that comes after it and from it.

So, the Good also is sovereign over this power. It is not in need of that which comes from it, but removing

16 See Plato, *Republic* 505d5–e1.

entirely everything that comes from it, and needing nothing of that, it is identical with what it was before it produced that. This is so since it would not have mattered to it if that had not come to be, | just as it was not going to begrudge being to anything that was able to come to be from it. As it is, there is nothing left that can come to be. For there is nothing which has not come to be, given that everything has come to be. But it itself was not all things in a way such that it would need them, and since it transcends all things, it was able to produce them and leave them to themselves while it | was over them.

13. But since it is the Good and not good, it must have had nothing in itself, since it did not even have the [property of being] good. For what it will have, it will have either as good or not good. But that which is not good will not be in that which is primarily and authoritatively the Good; nor will the Good | have the good [as a property]. If, then, the Good has neither that which is not good nor that which is good, it has nothing. If, then, it has nothing, it is "alone and isolated"[17] from other things. If, then, the other things are either goods and so not *the* Good, or are not goods, it will have neither of these properties; in not having them, it is the Good by having nothing. If, then, someone | adds something to it, either essence or intellect

17 See Plato, *Philebus* 63b7–8.

or the property of being beautiful, by that addition he subtracts from it the Good that it is.

Therefore, removing everything from it, and saying nothing about it, nor making a false claim about there being something in it, one allows the "is," not giving false testimony about things being present in it as do those who produce panegyrics with no knowledge in them and who reduce | the fame of the things they are praising by attributing to them less than their worth, being at a loss to say true things about the subjects behind the words. Then we, too, should try not to add anything of that which comes later and that which is lesser, but treat it as that cause which is above these things, while | not being identical to them.

For, again, it is the nature of the Good not to be all things nor to be any one of them. For if it were, it would fall under one identical [genus] to which they all belong. But by falling under one identical [genus] with all those, it could differ from them only by a unique differentia, and differentiation is addition. Then, it would be two, not one, of which one part is not good, namely, that which is common to other things, and one part good. | Therefore, it will be a mixture of good and not good. Therefore, it will not be purely nor primarily good; rather, that will be primarily good which, being other than the common part, is that by participating in which it has become good. But, then, the Good will be good by partaking. But that in which it partook is not one among all things; therefore, the Good is not one among all things. But if the Good, thus conceived, was in it |—for there was a differentia in virtue of which the composite was good—it is necessary for this to come from something else. But it was simple and uniquely good. Therefore, much more so is that from which it came uniquely good.

Therefore, that which is primarily good, that is, that which *is* the Good, reveals itself to us as being over all beings and uniquely good and having nothing in itself, | but unmixed with anything and over everything and the cause of everything. For neither that which is beautiful nor real beings come from what is evil nor, indeed, from that which is indifferent. For that which produces is better than that which is produced. For it is more perfect.

Commentary

THE TITLE OF THE TREATISE in Porphyry's list of the works of Plotinus found in his *Life of Plotinus* (5.30–31) is "That the Intelligibles (*ta noēta*) are not External to the Intellect, and on the Good." However, in the *summarium* of the treatises contained in *Ennead* V in HS, the title substitutes the word "concepts" (*ta noēmata*) for "intelligibles." Porphyry, in the *Life* (18.10–11), says that he wrote a work against Plotinus arguing that "concepts" *were* external to the intellect. Plotinus had this work read to him and delegated his disciple, Amelius, to write a reply. This view may also have been shared by Plotinus' fellow student Longinus (c. 213–272). See *Life* 20.89–95; cf. Proclus, *In Timaeum* 1.322.24). According to Porphyry's account, after a series of interchanges, he came to see the truth of Plotinus' doctrine. He even suggests that it was he, Porphyry, who urged Plotinus to write down the arguments for the doctrine, presumably, the work that constitutes part of V.5. Cf. III.9.1, 8 for another clear rejection of the externality of intelligibles. The distinction between *noēma* and *noēton* may not, by the time of Plotinus, be as sharp as it apparently was for Plato. In *Parmenides* 132b4, Socrates suggests that a Form may be a *noēma* "existing nowhere but in souls," that is, in intellects. Parmenides has no difficulty showing him that a Form cannot be a real "one over many" if it is only a *noēma*, and not that which a *noēma* is *of*, namely, an object of intellection, *to nooumenon* (c6–7). This term is not elsewhere used in Plato. Aristotle uses *to nooumenon* to refer to a *noēton* when it is considered, not in itself, but in relation to the intellect that is cognizing it. See, e.g., *On the Soul (De Anima)* 3.4.430a4; *Metaphysics* 12.9.1074a30, 1075a6.

Plotinus frequently appeals to the authority of Parmenides for support for his doctrine regarding the internality of the intelligibles. See *Parmenides*, B3 DK: "for the identical thing is there for thinking and for being (*to gar auto noein estin te kai einai*)." Cf. V.9.5, 29–30; V.1.8, 17–18; V.6.6, 22–23; III.8.8, 8; VI.7.41, 18; I.4.10, 6; III.5.7, 51. Plotinus evinces no doubt about the correct interpretation of this fragment.

Among Middle Platonists, we find a tendency to conflate *noēma* and *noēton* when the intelligible is being considered as virtually identical to a concept in the mind of God. See Alcinous, *Didaskalikos* 163.33, 164.30 Whittaker. But Alcinous can still retain the distinction between *noēton* and *noēma* when the latter is found in an intellect other than that of God, such as the soul of the universe. See

169.41–42. We may suppose that Porphyry was inclined to ignore the distinction between *noēma* and *noēton* as did the Middle Platonists, since the issue as reflected in this treatise concerns eternal Intellect. This does not resolve the issue, as Plotinus will explain. We cannot legitimately reject the externality of the intelligible on the grounds that, for Intellect, intelligible and concept are equivalent. Even if this were the case, we might well raise the question of whether what is in the Intellect is some sort of representation that is other than the intelligible/concept. See Pépin (1956) and Armstrong (1960) for some of the relevant historical evidence regarding Plotinus' consideration of the problem of the relation of intelligibles to a divine intellect.

Chapter 1

Plotinus introduces the question of how Intellect is related to intelligibles. He argues that if intelligibles are external to Intellect, then Intellect will not possess the truth but only a representation of it. Yet if Intellect does not possess truth, then nothing does and truth does not exist.

1, 1 *true and real intellect*: This is a reference to the "hypostasis" or principle of Intellect. For Plotinus, Intellect is the systematic expression of Plato's Demiurge and Aristotle's Unmoved Mover. But contrary to Middle Platonists like Alcinous, Intellect/Demiurge/Unmoved Mover are not conflated with the first principle of all, the Idea of the Good or the One. See Alcinous, *Didaskalikos* 164.29–165.4 Whittaker, for the explicit conflation. The term "real" does not imply that individual intellects or embodied intellects are not real, but rather that they are only images of the paradigm that Intellect is. The term "true" here seems to be used synonymously with "real." Thus, we might translate the words *ton alēthē noun kai ontōs* as "true or real Intellect."

Below it will be important to distinguish "ontological truth" from "semantic truth," the former being a property of being and the latter being a property of propositions. As it will turn out, it is ontological truth that must be identical with "true Intellect." See Beierwaltes (1991, 195).

1, 2 *will ever be . . . that are not*: The argument will show that Intellect cannot be in error or have false beliefs; indeed, Intellect cannot have any beliefs (*doxai*) at all. But here Plotinus is acknowledging that since false belief is manifestly a reality, and that it can only occur in subjects with intellects, it might also seem possible that the paradigm of intellection is susceptible to false beliefs, too. The thinking and saying "things that are not" is what Plato in *Sophist* 240cff. aims to show is of the essence of sophistry. The argument concludes (263d) by showing that thinking or saying falsities amounts to thinking or saying something "different from the things that are." It amounts to having false beliefs or expressing false beliefs about the subjects of propositions. The *Theaetetus* (187cff.) has already addressed the question of how false belief is even possible. The conclusion of that argument is that *if* knowledge is *true* belief, then *false* belief is impossible. But since false belief is possible, true belief is not knowledge. This is so because of the nature of knowledge (*epistēmē*) according to the two criteria laid down at 152c5–6, namely, that knowledge must be (a) infallible (*apseudes*) and must be (b) "of that which is" (*tou ontos*). The possibility of false belief would not defeat the definition of knowledge as true belief unless true belief failed to meet (b), since *true* belief can be stipulated to meet (a). But it would seem to be arbitrary to claim that true belief fails to meet (b) on the grounds that "that which is" refers exclusively to that which belief cannot attain to, namely, separate, immaterial Forms. One might thus suppose that even if there is knowledge of Forms, there is also knowledge of sensibles and that if true belief alone is not exactly what this knowledge is, true belief "plus" some additional "factor" will amount to knowledge. Plotinus, as the argument progresses, rejects this understanding of *Theaetetus*. The reason true belief does not attain to what is is exactly the reason why true belief cannot, after all, be infallible. The very fact that one can have false belief about something about which one has true belief entails that the true belief, though, true, is not infallible. Adventitiously having the truth, we might say, amounts to not having it at all. Compare the following. We sometimes say as a joke that even a broken clock is right twice a day. But is this correct? If the clock "says" three o'clock when it is in fact three o'clock, does the coincidence amount to "having" the right time? One might suppose so, but it is difficult to maintain that when we see that a properly functioning atomic clock says that it is three o'clock and a broken clock says that it is three o'clock, we are using "says" univocally. See further below.

1, 3 *unthinking*: The verb *anoētainōn* is rare in Plotinus. Besides here, it occurs only at II.9.1, 50. The rhetorical question suggests that if Intellect were "in error" or "had beliefs about the things that are not" then it would not be engaging in thinking. Thus, "thinking" for Plotinus indicates a specific activity; having beliefs, whether true or false, would not be acts of thinking. This use corresponds to Plato's use of *noēsis* in *Republic* 511d8 for the mode of cognition at the highest section of the Divided Line. But cf. 534a2, where *noēsis* is used to include cognition at both of the sections of the top part of the Divided Line, *epistēmē* and *dianoia*. That there is no *dianoia* or discursive reasoning in Intellect will become clear below. Discursive reasoning belongs only to embodied human beings. Cf. V.3.3, 35–37. Plotinus will, therefore, use "intellection" or "thinking" and "knowledge" interchangeably in some contexts.

See Emilsson (2007, ch. 4) on discursive and non-discursive thought in Plotinus and the dependence of the former on the latter.

1, 3–6 *It must, therefore, . . . at second hand*: The word for "know" here *eidenai*, is being used generically for "cognition." The conclusions being drawn, namely, that Intellect does not forget, does not employ images, or cognize ambiguously, or at second hand, are proposed as properties of *noēsis*. The word *amphibolon* ("ambiguously") indicates fallible cognition wherein there is no entailment from "S is in a cognitive mental state" to "S has the truth." The case would be similar if S has to recall what it knows, is employing images, or is cognizing information obtained second hand. What all these share is indirectness or mediacy, rather than the directness of *noēsis*.

1, 6–8 *So, then, its knowledge . . . self-evident to it*: Plotinus turns to the possibility that Intellect could know through demonstration (*apodeixis*). Cf. V.8.7, 43. Aristotle, *Posterior Analytics* 1.2.71b16–23, defines a demonstration as a type of syllogism in which the conclusion is known through its cause(s). Demonstrative knowledge of p is knowledge of why p is true. Even if demonstrative knowledge were infallible, having it would involve mediation through the premises. As Aristotle points out in the lines following the above passage, the premises must be (1) true, (2) primary, (3) immediate, (4) more known than the conclusion, (5) prior to and (6) causes of the conclusion. Here Plotinus is focusing on (4). So, even if there were *noēsis* of conclusions of syllogisms, there would have to be *noēsis* of the premises and that would have to be immediate.

1, 8 *self-evident* (*enargē*): The word is usually translated as "clear." But this is ambiguous between an objective and a subjective property. Cf. Aristotle, *Physics* 1.1.184a1–21, who distinguishes things clearer (*saphestera*) by nature and things clearer to us. At V.1.2, 28, Plotinus seems to use *enargestera* and *phanerōtera* synonymously. See below 2, 15, where Plotinus says that it is *enargēs* to Intellect that it is in the state that it is, namely, the state of knowing. For Plotinus, "clearer by nature" and "clearer to us" would coincide in Intellect. Its objects are the clearest possible and it possesses perfect clarity or perhaps transparency with regard to these objects. Since Intellect is identical with them, what is self-evident to it is its own self.

1, 8–9 *Actually, our argument . . . those that are not*: Here Plotinus claims that there is no way to distinguish *noēsis* of the premises from a putative *noēsis* of the conclusion, though he does not say why. Perhaps the reasoning is something like this. If Intellect has demonstrative knowledge, that knowledge is of the truth of propositions. Either Intellect sees all at once the connection between the truth of the conclusion and the truth of the premises or it does not. If it does, then that is just as immediate or evident to it as is the truth of the premises, that is, there would be no way to distinguish between immediate *noēsis* of the premises and a supposed mediate *noēsis* of the conclusion. If it does not, then the conclusion is not immediate to it and infallibility is foregone.

Kühn (2009, 163) refers to Alexander of Aphrodisias, *On Aristotle Prior Analytics* 54.18–20, where Alexander notes that in a first figure syllogism, the conclusion becomes immediately self-evident (*autothen enargēs*) by the premises.

1, 9–11 *But as for . . . self-evident comes?:* This argument is usually taken as directed against the Epicureans, since the term for self-evidence, *enargeia*, is thematized by Epicurus himself, according to the report of Sextus Empiricus, *Against the Professors* 7.203. But the same argument would apply to anyone who wanted to differentiate immediate and mediate *noēsis*. Behind Plotinus' question is the position he is working towards in this treatise, namely, that intelligibles are not external to Intellect. If self-evidence "comes to Intellect" from anywhere, then it is the result of an experience or mental event of some sort. But in that case, the mental event is itself only a representation of the object of *noēsis*. Then, Intellect would not have the truth. What would be self-evident to it would be only the basis for an inference to the truth. Perhaps Plotinus focuses on Epicurus because for him self-evidence is found in sense-perception and the general tenor of Plotinus' argument is clearest in the case of sense-perception.

1, 11–12 *And from where . . . self-evident to it*: The term "conviction" (*pistis*) is also Epicurean, though it is widely used by Academics, Peripatetics, and Stoics, too. For the Epicurean expression of the argument for the self-evident see Diogenes Laertius 10.32. The words "from where" indicate that conviction is supposed to arise from something else, whether that be a mental event or some extra-mental event or both. But, once again, "being convinced" or "being in a confident state" is not having the truth about which one is supposedly confident. To be confident "that such and such is the case" is perforce to distinguish the confidence from the truth.

Sextus Empiricus, *Outlines of Pyrrhonism* 2.169–170 and *Against the Professors* 7.364 provides the clearest expression of the issue Plotinus is addressing. In the first passage, Sextus attacks demonstrative knowledge along the same lines as Plotinus. An argument which infers a non-evident conclusion from evident premises should admit that the conclusion qua conclusion and the premises qua premises are relative, that is, they are grasped together. But then either the conclusion is evident or the premises are non-evident. If this is so, then there is no non-evident knowledge inferable from evident premises. In the second passage, Sextus challenges the possibility of self-evidence. He argues, like Plotinus in his argument against Epicurus, that the mental state of a perceiver is necessarily other than the object of that mental state, namely, the perceptible. And then, the supposed self-evidence is really the basis for an inference from the mental state to the supposed truth. As Sextus says (365), "nothing is of a nature to be perceived of itself (*ex heautou*)," that is, nothing that is perceived can also be the content of the mental state of the perceiver. There is an irreducible or ineliminable inference from the one to the other. So, there is no such thing as self-evidence. It is useful here to draw on a distinction little used in contemporary philosophy, that between certainty and certitude. The former is equivalent to "infallibility," the absolute impossibility of error; the latter is a purely subjective state which implies nothing about how the world is. Certitude might lead someone to die for a cause, but that certitude obviously does not guarantee the truth of the claims constitutive of that cause.

Why is this so important both to Sextus and to Plotinus? After all, one might maintain that certainty or infallibility about anything is impossible and though this might be a cause for regret it is not disastrous. If infallible cognition is not possible or even if it is exceedingly rare, we can still have demonstrations and non-demonstrative conclusions that are reasonable and, indeed, even reasonably certain. Sextus and Plotinus reject this view for the identical reason, namely, that there is no such thing as non-infallible knowledge. If infallible knowledge does not exist, then there is no such thing as knowledge just because there is no fallible knowledge. To this remarkable claim, one might well reply that if knowledge is impossible, then there is something else, whatever we may choose to call it, that is almost as good. Consider the following comparison. One might come to believe that immortality is not on the cards for human beings, but this fact does not preclude the possibility of a long and happy life nor should it undermine any effort to prolong one's life as much as possible.

Sextus' argument in the passages above assume the radical Pyrrhonian position, namely, that if nothing is self-evident, then there is no *reason* to believe anything rather than its opposite. This is so because anything we believe that is not self-evident is either believed for no reason at all or for some reason. If the former, then there is literally no more reason to believe it rather than its opposite. But if the latter, then our putative reasons or evidence are only real if they entail that for which they are evidence. But they cannot do this if there is no such thing as self-evident knowledge, that is, it would not be self-evident to us that there was in fact an entailment. And without entailment, the notion of "non-entailing evidence" is completely obscure and, ultimately, incoherent.

Plotinus, like Sextus, believes that infallibility is a property of knowledge. More precisely, he believes that it is a property of the highest form of cognition, the *ne plus ultra* of cognition, the *noēsis* of Intellect. Once he has established that infallible knowledge is possible and that it actually exists, Plotinus will go on to argue in other treatises that, for various forms of embodied cognition, the existence of infallible knowledge stands as a bulwark against the sweeping sceptical claim that without such knowledge, total suspension of belief is the only rational course of action. In the present treatise, to grant the claim that intelligibles are external to Intellect is thereby to grant that nothing is self-evident to Intellect and that therefore it has no knowledge. If Intellect, or at least *some* intellect, is bereft of knowledge, then not only is knowledge impossible for embodied human beings, but reason and philosophy itself are rendered impotent.

1, 12–15 *For even sensibles . . . judgments about them*: According to Sextus, *Against the Professors* 7.2–3, 8.9, Epicurus held that "all sensibles are true and real" meaning that the sensible cannot be other than as it appears. When error or misapprehension does occur, it is owing to the beliefs or opinions (*doxai*) one has in regard to these (cf. 7.210). Plotinus insists that the claim that all sensibles are true and real can be distilled to yield no more than "apparent existence" (*dokousan hupostasin*). And like Sextus, Plotinus argues that there is an inferential gap between the apparent and the real. This must be so, since from the claim that "x is apparently thus and so" only a disjunct follows: either the appearance is of the real, that is, extra-mental existent, *or* it is of the one who is having the experience ("it appears to me this way because of the state of my body"). So, we cannot infer real existence from apparent existence. So, if Intellect has self-evident knowledge, it cannot arise from sense-perception. Accordingly, one needs intellect or discursive reasoning to be able to make the correct inference. Contrary to Epicurus, the immediacy of sense-perception is the wrong sort of immediacy. It does not necessarily result from contact with the extra-mental real as opposed to subjective mental states. The premise of this argument that is hitherto suppressed is that the only sort of immediacy that is a property of knowledge is that which does necessarily result from contact with the real. That is why it will turn out that intelligibles are not external to the Intellect. The reality of that which is external is always inferred from a cognitive state and no such inference is infallible. Epicurus holds that every "presentation" (*phantasia*) is, qua presentation, something that is "evidence" (*enargeia*). If Epicurus is correct, then from the shared claim that knowledge is infallible, we could not go on to infer that that which is knowable, namely, intelligibles, must be internal to the Intellect. Thus, sensibles are evident, though external, so the putative intelligibles, even if they are evident, need not be so.

1, 15–19 *For even if . . . object remains external*: This argument provisionally concedes that the apparently real is in fact in the external object and not in the subject. Cf. Sextus Empiricus, *Outlines of Pyrrhonism* 2.51, for a parallel argument. Even with this concession, what sense-perception cognizes is only a reflected representation (*eidōlon*) of that external object. The term *eidōlon*, which is also sometimes translated "image," indicates in general something that is derived from a higher principle and hence, according to Plotinus' metaphysical principles, always diminished in intelligibility. Although the content of sense-perception is an image of the external object, sense-perception itself is an image of intellection. See I.1.7, 12. The English word "image" sometimes has the connotation of a human made copy of something else, for example, a drawing. But the primary connotation of *eidōlon* is "derivation from above" not from "below." Consequently, an *eidōlon* will always have a sort of derivative sameness with that which it represents. Cf. Plato, *Sophist* 240a7–8. Sameness alone might suggest that possessing a representation of truth would be equivalent to having truth itself. But because an *eidōlon* is always derived and so inferior, this is not the case. No *eidōlon* is equivalent to that which it represents. Hence, possessing it cannot in principle amount to possessing truth.

1, 17 *apprehension* (*antilēpsis*): This is Plotinus' general term for the result of some cognitive act, whether this be perception of proper or common sensibles, memory, or some intelligible content. Cf. I.4.10, 4–6; IV.3.23, 31; IV.3.30, 11–14; V.1.12, 13; VI.7.7, 25–27, etc.

1, 19 *external* (*exō*): From the fact that what is possessed is a representation, that of which it is a representation must remain external. Plotinus seems to take this as a matter of logic. If B represents A, then the cognitive possession of B entails the externality of A. "External" clearly means something other than "distinct from." For all intelligibles known by Intellect are really distinct from each other, though none are therefore "external" to each other or to Intellect. Given that an *eidōlon* is always ontologically posterior to its source, I suggest that "external" means "ontologically prior to." Aristotle, *Metaphysics* 5.11.1019a1–4, says that Plato used this sense of "prior," indicating that if A can exist without B but not vice versa, then A is prior "according to nature or being" (*ousia*). W. D. Ross, in his commentary on Aristotle's *Metaphysics* (vol. 1, 317), notes that there is no passage in the dialogues in which "prior" is used in this way. "Aristotle," says Ross, "is thinking doubtless of an oral utterance of his master."

1, 20–21 *Given that when . . . connect with them*: If the objects of Intellect's knowledge are other than it, what it knows will be other than intelligibles. The assumption here is that the object of knowledge must not be other than the knower. The analogy with the above argument concerning sense-perception is clear: just as sense-perception only "connects with" (*suntuchoi*) an *eidōlon* of sensible objects, so if intelligibles were other than Intellect, it would only connect with an *eidōlon* of intelligibles.

Plato, *Theaetetus* 197b–d, distinguishes between "possessing" (*409ktēsthai*) knowledge and "having" (*echein*) it. This is, roughly, the distinction between (a) the presence of the intelligible to the intellect, and (b) the awareness of that presence. Clearly, we can conceive of cases where (a) holds and (b) does not, for example, cases in which we know (a) something but we have (b) forgotten it. As Plato goes on to argue, 199b, it is (b) rather than (a) that deserves to be called "knowledge" in the primary sense, because only in the case of (b) is one without error (*apseudein*) and connected to what is (7–8). These are the two criteria for knowledge set out at 152c5–6. Plotinus follows Plato in making "having" knowledge prior in definition to "possessing" it. But the putative case of knowledge that Plato is discussing in this passage, namely, true propositional belief, is in fact later shown not to be knowledge at all. Intellect, wherein knowledge primarily resides, cannot "possess" knowledge at all, that is, cannot have the intelligibles present without also being aware of their presence. In that case, the distinction between "possessing" and "having" collapses.

1, 20 *intelligibles* (*noēta*): *LSJ* defines *noēton* as "falling within the province of the mental (*nous*)" as opposed to the visible or sensible. This is exactly correct, but cannot serve as a translation. Translating the term *noēton* as used by Plotinus as "intelligible" brings with it a certain crucial ambiguity. It suggests a passive potency in the being cognized, one which might or might not be actualized. Thus, being can be intelligible and never actually cognized or "intellected." But Plotinus thinks in fact that this is only a logical possibility derived from the distinction between being and its property, intelligibility. So, in a sense, there is nothing that is intelligible for Plotinus if that means it can be cognized but in fact is not. As we shall see below (ll.65–68), taking "intelligible" in this way can lead one to misconstrue Plotinus' arguments against the externality and for the internality of intelligibles. Of course, an intelligible may be only potentially intelligible to a particular embodied individual.

1, 21 *connect with* (*suntuchoi*): Cf. Plato, *Theaetetus* 186c7–10, where the definition of knowledge (*epistēmē*) as sense-perception is finally refuted. Socrates says that it is not possible to "hit upon" (*tuchein*) the truth if one does not hit upon being (*ousia*). And if one fails to hit upon truth, one does not know. The prefix *sun-* here indicates the unity that occurs when there is a "connection" between Intellect and intelligible or truth. The Platonic point regarding the unity of an intellect and intelligible for knowledge to occur is thematized by Aristotle. See *On the Soul* (*De Anima*)

3.4.430a4–5; 3.5.430a19–20; 3.6.430b25–26; 3.7.431b17; 3.8.431a22–23. Cf. *Metaphysics* 12.9.1074b38–1075a5. The metaphor of "connecting" may be compared with the metaphor of "touching" (*thigganein*) used similarly by Aristotle, *Metaphysics* 9.10.1051b25.

1, 21–23 *For it is . . . have the knowledge*: What sort of possibility is this? Presumably, the *gar* ("for") is an explanation of the previous line. Plotinus seems to be drawing the consequence of intelligibles being other than Intellect. If they are other, then Intellect may or may not connect with them. Eliminating this as a possibility would mean eliminating the otherness. Eliminating the otherness would mean that Intellect is eternally in contact with intelligibles, that is, they are not external to it.

1, 23–24 *But if they . . . term "linked" mean*: Literally, "yoked together." Plotinus is perhaps alluding to an unknown opponent who used this term to indicate that an intelligible is related to an intellect. The metaphor of yoking suggesting some sort of union short of identity. If, though, this relation does not establish identity, then the metaphor employed is completely unilluminating. Perhaps this is an oblique reference to followers of Longinus, of whom Porphyry had been one.

1, 24–25 *And in that . . . will be impressions*: The term "impression" (*tupos*) is Stoic; it does not appear in the Epicurean texts. Diogenes Laertius 7.45, reports the Stoics as holding that a "'presentation' (*phantasia*) is an impression in the soul, the name being appropriately transferred from the imprints in wax made by a seal-ring." Plotinus may or may not have the Stoics in mind here. As he says at V.9.5, 21–23, the objects of Intellect's thinking cannot be impressions coming from something else, but paradigms (*archetupa*), that is, primary beings, and the substance of Intellect. It seems that *tupos* is being taken as in a way the genus of which *noēma* is a species and Plotinus has in mind *Parmenides* 132b4 mentioned above. Even if a *tupos* accurately represents what it is a *tupos* of, it cannot be the truth it represents. The entire plausibility of this line of thinking depends upon "truth" being understood here ontologically and not semantically. For if truth is understood in the latter way, then the claim that no representation is true amounts to the strange claim that there cannot be true propositions.

1, 24 *acts of intellection* (*noēseis*): The plural is odd, since there are no multiple acts of intellection in Intellect. At V.9.7, 14 Plotinus denies that Forms are *noēseis* for the reason that an act of intellection might be taken to bring into being that which is its intentional object. But Forms are prior in being to being thought; they are the product of the One. This passage seems to be the only place in which *noēseis* is being used of Intellect. Perhaps Plotinus is making a general point, because even for human beings, intellection does not have as its object impressions. See also V.9.9, 11.

1, 25 *And if this . . . they are impacts*: If acts of intellection are impressions, then they act externally since an impression is of something that is external. The term "impacts" (*plēgai*) indicates the action of one body on another. Cf. III.1.2, 11; III.6.6, 35, 62, etc. The point seems to be that if intelligibles are external to Intellect, the *only* way that representations of these could be present to Intellect would be by a physical event, an "impacting" of some sort. This possibility is ruled out by the immateriality of intelligibles. At *Sophist* 246e–248a, the Eleatic Stranger refutes the "reformed" materialists who agree that there are at least some things, e.g., moral qualities, that are not material. The recalcitrant materialists will not admit even this. If, for example, everything intelligible is a body, as the Stoics hold, then knowledge, if it exists, would have to be the result of some sort of "impact." If it can be shown that intelligibles cannot be bodies, and if intelligibles are what is known, then, if knowledge exists, it is not the result of such impacts. A parallel argument can be marshaled for the immateriality of intellect. Cf. Aristotle, *On the Soul (De Anima)* 3.4.429a24–29.

1, 25–26 *But how will . . . of such things*: If acts of intellection are the result of impacts, what is needed is an account of the physical process of impaction. In particular, an impact must produce a particular shape (*morphē*). Plotinus obviously thinks that this is an absurd result, no doubt because most intelligibles do not have shapes, including smells, sounds, etc. Cf. Alexander of Aphrodisias, *On the Soul* (*De Anima)* 72.5–11 Bruns, who gives a similar argument. Furthermore, and more profoundly, any physical shape will have particular dimensions. But knowledge of a kind of shape or of shape in general cannot be equivalent to knowledge of a particular dimension. That is why Aristotle insists that knowledge is of the universal. See *Posterior Analytics* 1.31.87b38–39.

1, 26–27 *And in that . . . just like sense-perception*: Aristotle, *On the Soul* (*De Anima)* 3.4.429a13–18, concedes that thinking is analogous to sense-perception, though as he goes on to argue, a29–31, the sense in which the faculty of sense-perception and intellect are "impassive" (*apathes*) is different. At *Metaphysics* 4.5.1009b12–17, Aristotle includes Democritus, Empedocles, and other materialists among those who believe that thinking (*phronēsis*) and sense-perception are identical and that they are an "alteration" (*alloiōsis*), that is, a physical change in the soul. I take it that Plotinus is here referencing the general Aristotelian argument against a physicalist account of thinking, in particular pointing out that if intellection is like sense-perception, then the object of intellection must be external, for like the perceptible, it produces an alteration in the soul.

1, 27–30 *And in what . . . beautiful or just?*: Plotinus here asks three rhetorical questions raised against the hypothesis that intellection is identical with sense-perception: (1) how will the apprehension in intellection be different from that in sense-perception except in that the former will apprehend smaller objects; (2) how can the knower know that it has apprehended correctly; (3) how can it know that the object apprehended has a property like being good or beautiful or just? As for (1), I take it that Epicurus is the target. See Diogenes Laertius 10.49, quoting *Letter to Herodotus.* Epicurus says that the atoms responsible for our cognition and coming from external objects enter the senses or the intellect according to the size and fit of their effluences. Plotinus seems to be supposing that the size of the shape grasped by an intellect would be smaller than that of the shape perceived, suggesting perhaps that if it were larger, it, too, would be perceived.

(2) raises a much deeper problem for Plotinus' opponents. If apprehension is of representations, what is the basis for claiming that what is apprehended correctly represents what is external. This is, again, the inference problem. So long as there is an indirect inference (via some additional premise)

to be made from "S apprehends p" to "p accurately represents P," there can be no infallibility or certainty. As Plato argues in *Theaetetus* 187aff., if true belief is knowledge, then false belief is not possible; if false belief is possible, then true belief is not knowledge. But the possibility that one apprehends incorrectly (has a false belief) means that apprehending correctly is not knowledge. This is so precisely because the apprehension does not guarantee its own truth. So long as we accept that the object of knowledge is external, attempts to meet this objection will inevitably amount to a search for criteria for correct apprehension. But these criteria will focus on how the external object is "presented" or affects the putative knower. This is the approach of the Academic Sceptic Carneades. See Sextus, *Against the Professors* 7.150–189. Such external criteria obviously cannot bridge the inferential gap. For it is always possible to ask, given the presence of the criteria, whether things are really as they appear.

(3) presumes that the grasp of moral qualities is second-order cognition. That is, if something is perceived, it is a further act of cognition to judge that this thing is good or beautiful. It is not another act of sense-perception.

1, 30–32 *For each of . . . will be there*: This line presumably provides the reason why the apprehension of moral qualities cannot come through sense-perception. But the words "other than the object" (*allo autou*) are ambiguous and can be understood, as by Armstrong, as "other than it." In the next line, *autōi* probably refers to the cognizer not the object, supporting Armstrong's interpretation. It seems that the point is identical in either case, namely, that the moral qualities will be external and so the truth in their cases will be with them.

1, 31 *principles of judgment* (*hai tēs kriseōs archai*): This probably refers to the Forms themselves which are the principles for judging whether something is good, beautiful, just, etc. The words "the truth will be there" indicate clearly that it is ontological truth that is at issue here.

1, 32 *The truth will be there* (*ekei*): The ordinary word *ekei* ("there") is almost always used by Plotinus to refer to the intelligible world, "yonder," so to speak. In a more specific context, "the truth is there" would certainly indicate the intelligible realm and Intellect. Here, it need only mean that wherever the principles of judgment are, they are external to the intellect, according to those who hold that intellection is, like sense-perception, of externals.

1, 32–33 *And then, either . . . do have intellect*: Plotinus thinks the second alternative is true: the intelligibles are not without sense-perception, life, and intellect. He is no doubt thinking of Plato's *Sophist* 248e6–249a2, where the

Eleatic Stranger asks the rhetorical question: "Are we really going to be persuaded that motion (*kinēsis*), life (*zōē*), soul (*psychē*), and intelligence (*phronēsis*) are not present to the perfectly real (*tōi pantelōs onti*), nor that it itself is alive and is intelligent, but stands immutable in holy solemnity, having no intellect (*noun*)?" This is a foundational text for all later Platonists, though its precise meaning is much disputed. Two crucial questions are: (1) what is the scope of "the perfectly real" and (2) what does it mean to include motion, life, etc., within the perfectly real?

Plotinus' answer to the first question is that "the perfectly real" refers to the hypostasis Intellect, which is identical with intelligibles. Cf. *Republic* 477a3 on "the perfectly real" being perfectly knowable. Cf. VI.7.8, 25–27, where the language is slightly different. Intellect does not have the perfect unity (*hen pantelōs einai*) of the One, but it is perfect (*teleos*) Intellect and perfect life. The second question then seems to become the question: is just Intellect alive, etc. or are Forms alive, too? Some have thought that the latter alternative is correct, relying on V.9.8, 1–4: *Ei oun hē noēsis enontos, ekeino to eidos to enon, kai hē idea autē. Ti oun touto: nous kai hē noera ousia, ouch hetera tou nou hekastē idea, all' hekastē nous. Kai holos men ho nous ta panta eidē, hekaston de eidos nous hekastos*. Armstrong translates: "If, then, the thought [of Intellect] is of what is within it, that which is within it is its immanent form, and this is the Idea. What then is this? Intellect and the intelligent substance; each individual Idea is not other than Intellect, but each is Intellect. *And Intellect as a whole is all the Forms, and each individual Form is an individual intellect"* (my emphasis). Fronterotta translates, "Si donc l'intellection est l'intellection d'une chose qui se trouve à l'intérieur de l'Intellect, cette chose est une Form, c'est l'Idée elle-même. -De quoi s'agit-il donc? -De l'Intellect, de la réalité intellectuelle. Chaque idée n'est pas différente de l'Intellect, mais chacune est elle-même Intellect. *Et l'Intellect dans sa totalité est toutes les Formes, et chaque Forme est un intellect"* (my emphasis). Both of these translations take the crucial phrase *hekaston de eidos nous hekastos* to mean that each Form is itself an intellect, not as the text literally says, "each Form is each intellect." MacKenna translates, "If, then, the Intellection is an act upon the inner content (of the Intellectual-Principle), that content is the Form, and the Form is the Idea. What, then, is that content? An Intellectual-Principle and an Intellective Essence, no Idea distinguishable from the Intellectual-Principle, each actually being that Principle. *The Intellectual-Principle entire is the total of the Ideas, and each of them is the (entire) Intellectual-Principle in a special form"* (my emphasis). MacKenna is closer to the idea being conveyed, though the words "*each of them is the (entire) Intellectual-Principle in a special form"* are more of a gloss than a translation. In the lines following, 5–7, Plotinus compares all the Forms to a "whole body of knowledge" and each Form to a theorem within that body of knowledge. Each is a part of the whole in the sense that it has a particular power. But the whole body of knowledge is identical with Intellect.

Taking the text literally, we need only conclude that Plotinus wants to say that Intellect is cognitively identical with all the Forms and that each Form is Intellect and each individual intellect, that is, each of the undescended intellects of human beings. The words "each individual Form is an individual intellect," taken in the most straightforward way, suggests either that the Form *has* an intellect apart from the intellect(s) that are thinking it, or that it is an intellect thinking itself. Neither of these makes any sense or is true to the text. At III.8.9, 12–13, Plotinus says that Intellect and intelligible are coupled, meaning that the intelligible is internal to Intellect. As we shall see, that internality is cognitive identity, the "having" of the intelligible as opposed to the mere "possessing" of it. See above, comm. on 20–21. So, it is correct to say that the intelligible thinks, but only in the sense that the intelligible is identical with that which thinks. There are no grounds for concluding that in addition to the thinking of Intellect and individual intellects that there is additional thinking going on in the intelligible world, namely, the thinking engaged in by the intelligibles.

1, 32 *without sense-perception* (*anaisthēta*): Plotinus does not think that Intellect or Forms literally have sense-perception. He argues that sense-perception must exist in the intelligible world but only as an intelligible paradigm. See V.8.12, 15.

1, 33–37 *And if they . . . are they related?*: Truth, that is, all intelligibles and Intellect are "simultaneously" (*hama*) in the intelligible world. Since the intelligible world is timeless, the simultaneity is a metaphor for mutual entailment. Alternatively, the simultaneity refers to what we as embodied intellects discover simultaneously when we attain to the intelligible world. If we contemplate a Form supposing it to be something like a lifeless shape, we can be certain that we are not in fact in touch with Forms, but only of images of them, the images that are words or concepts or symbols.

1, 35–36 *what the truth here is like* (*pōs echei hē entautha alētheia*): The answer to this question is given at 2, 18–24. Clearly, this is a question about ontological truth.

1, 36–37 *and whether the . . . are they related?*: The answer is given at 2, 1–13. Cf. III.8.9, 5–11. The answer to the question is fundamental to the theme of the treatise. If the intelligibles are not external to the Intellect, do they still remain *other* than the Intellect? If they are other, what

propositional claims that "that which is just is necessarily beautiful" or "a plane figure is inscribable in a circle" *could not* be true. The underlying assumption is based on what is claimed at *Phaedo* 105b8–c7 where Socrates says that he will forego the "safe" explanation for why something is hot, namely, that there is hotness in it, and now say that something is hot because there is fire in it and fire always brings with it hotness. So, the Form of Fire and the Form of Hotness are somehow necessarily connected. It seems that Plotinus is suggesting that if each Form were separate from each other, then Socrates' "cleverer hypothesis" could not be true. In *Sophist* 259e4–6, the Eleatic Stranger makes the stronger claim that the isolation (*dialuein*) of Forms would produce the abolition of discourse (*logos*). Accordingly, there must be a weaving (*sumplokē*) of Forms. What this weaving amounts to is a matter of controversy. English forces us to say "weaving" or perhaps "plaiting" rather than "interwoveness" which is more accurate. That which supposedly makes discourse possible is a permanent feature of the world of Forms; it is not something we do when we speak or think. Even the Demiurge or Intellect are not "weavers." The unity among Forms that Plotinus seeks to explicate is clearly an effort to cash out the metaphor of a *sumplokē*. The dispersal (*diespasmenon*) of Forms would be the negation of their *sumplokē*. If Forms were "unwoven,"not only could there be no necessary truths, but even contingent truths, insofar as they manifest a measure of intelligibility in instantiating more than one Form, would not be possible.

Plotinus takes the hypothesis of the simplicity of each Form as entailing the dispersal and denial of the weaving. Plato, *Symposium* 211b1, seems to take the Forms as being uniform (*monoeides*), evidently a sort of simplicity. At *Philebus* 15b1 he describes the Forms as "units" (*monades*), which certainly suggests simplicity. And, of course, the Forms are frequently referred to each as a "one over many." See *Parmenides* 132a1–4, *Republic* 596a6–7. How can the Form be both simple and not simple?

Plotinus' solution to this problem depends upon two claims. The first is that the One is unique in its absolute simplicity. See III.8.9, 17, where the One is said to be "most simple" (*haploustaton*). From this it follows that no Form can be absolutely simple in itself. The second is that the One is "virtually all things" (*dunamis tōn pantōn*). See III.8.10, 1. Cf. IV.8.6, 11; V.1. 7, 9–10; VI.9.5, 36. The technical term "virtually" or "virtuality" indicates that the One is all of its products in a superior mode of being. Since its products are everything there is, it is itself all things, analogous to the way "white" light is virtually all the colors of the spectrum. See VI.9.9, 1. So, the requisite unity for, say, Justice and Beauty in order to make it true that that which is just is beautiful is found in the cause of these

Forms, which is virtually both of them. The One unites these Forms thereby explaining how in a sense one Form is part of what another Form is.

But of course this cannot be the whole story because the One is also virtually all those Forms which are not woven together, at least not directly. For the One is virtually the Form of Three and the Form of Even, though it is false that any group that is three is even. This is why Intellect is an essential part of the system, irreducible to Forms or to the One. In desiring the One qua Good, Intellect "achieves" the object of its desire in the only way possible, by thinking all that is thinkable. On the hypothesis of the present treatise, this act of thinking amounts to the realization or actualization of itself. See V.1.7, 1–6. Thus, Intellect thinks the entire array of Forms as an articulated whole. The unity that grounds the truth of any necessary proposition is the unity of that whole. The unity considered in its cause is absolute unity; the unity considered "from below," that is, as we try to understand the truth of true necessary propositions, is that which makes all these propositions true. One reason why intelligibles must be internal to Intellect is that if they were external, the intelligible unity that each Form is would preclude it from being interwoven with any other. Each would be a little island of intelligibility. I leave out here the complication introduced by the "greatest kinds" (*megista genē*) of *Sophist* 254b–255e, Identity, Difference,

Motion, Rest, and Being. These do have a unifying effect, but only in the sense that one Form is, say, different from another owing to partaking in Difference. This, however, does not explain why anything that is just is beautiful. The entire treatise VI.2 is devoted to the examination of the categories of the intelligible world.

1, 43–49 *And where and . . . be sense-perception*: Plotinus now asks a series of rhetorical questions predicated on the notion that intelligibles are a series of dispersed simples. The intended absurdity of the questions results from taking seriously the idea that Forms are in place and that they can therefore be dispersed in different places. Apart from the first question, which asks for the "location" of each intelligible, the other questions focus on the absurdity of Intellect knowing the supposedly dispersed Forms. There would have to be something like discursivity in order for Intellect to know each one. In fact, at ll. 45–46, Intellect must "remain" (*menei*) "where" it is in order to be Intellect. Cf. *Timaeus* 42e5–6 where the Demiurge is said to "remain" (*menein*) in its appointed place after having produced the cosmos. The requisite discursivity for cognizing dispersed intelligibles is reflected in the Greek word *dianoia,* where the *dia* indicates some sort of succession for a *nous.* The reason why the intelligibles must be internal to Intellect is the same reason why there can be no *dianoia* in Intellect. If we take the intelligibles to be like golden statues, then

Intellect's knowledge of them will be like sense-perception, that is, it will not be identical with the object of knowledge but only with an image of it.

1, 49–50 *Further, why is . . . another something else?*: The question sounds obscure since it seems to presuppose the answer: why is x different from y, where "x" and "y" represent different things? At VI.7.2, 10–11 Plotinus says, "in the intelligible world, everything is in one thing, so that the thing (*to pragma*) and the 'why' (*dia ti*) of the thing are identical." The present question presumes the hypothesis that the Forms are dispersed and that they are not united in Intellect. For an intelligible entity, there is nothing to differentiate it from another. For example, what makes Triangularity different from Circularity? It cannot be that the first has a triangular shape and the second a circular one since intelligible entities do not have shapes. It is only in their being eternally thought as different that they can be so. But the thinking of them as different does not make them to be so. If that were the case, then thinking would be prior to being which Plotinus explicitly denies. See above on 1, 24. The One is virtually all the Forms. The multiplicity of Forms is how the One "looks" in its "external" activity which is that of Intellect. An important consequence, canvassed later in the treatise, is that the only way for something other than the One to "attain" it is for it to cognize its diverse products, the Forms.

As Proclus notes, *In Timaeum* 1.322.24–25, Porphyry held that the Forms are anterior to Intellect, and Longinus held that they are posterior. Proclus himself, 323.10–22, tries to accommodate (1) the fact that Forms are prior in being, and (2) that they are identical with Intellect. As Proclus puts it, the Forms are prior to Intellect "in the intelligible mode" (*noētōs*) and internal to Intellect "in the intellective mode" (*noerōs*). That is, we can think about Intellect either as the locus of intelligible content or as the eternal and paradigmatic activity of contemplating that content.

At *Timaeus* 30c2–31a1, Plato describes the "Living Animal" (*to zōon*) which contains all the paradigms to be used by the Demiurge in bringing intelligibility to the chaos of the receptacle. They are said to be "parts" (*moria*) of the whole. Plotinus, III.9.1, 14–15, specifies that these intelligible objects are internal to the Demiurge or Intellect, though he adds that at least there is nothing against taking the text in this way. Cf. V.1.8, 21. At VI.6.7, 16–17, he corrects the *Timaeus* language of parts and wholes (*ek pantōn*) to that of "encompassing" (*periechon*), no doubt resisting the thought that Forms have parts. But the central point is that the Forms must be interconnected if they are to provide the foundation for the intelligible connections here below, those such as classificatory connections, relational, entailment, etc. Intellect provides the only possibility of such interconnectedness. For example, in an Aristotelian framework, a species is related to a genus in the order of act to potency. So, to say that a man is an animal is to claim that the unity of the species is that of an actualized potentiality. This could not be the case in the intelligible world, where one Form is not in potency to another. So, how are the Forms of Animality and Humanity supposed to be related? It is the nature of Intellect to be these Forms in thinking them "simultaneously." The diversity yet connectedness between animality and humanity here below—given that there are animals that are not human—are among the ways that Intellect appears when nature is generated from Soul.

1, 50–54 *But the greatest . . . the true reality*: This seems to be a reprise of the arguments above. The externality of intelligibles entails that Intellect does not possess truth. Clearly, again, ontological truth is at issue here. The only way that Intellect can know the truth is by having it. Believing a true proposition does not amount to having truth. One may grant this claim if only on the grounds that knowing is defined as having truth. But Plotinus adds that if intelligibles are external, then Intellect would be "deceived" (*diepseusthai*) in "all the things" it contemplates. Does this follow? Plotinus evidently takes "contemplation" (*theōria*) as a sort of mental seeing requiring direct contact with the object contemplated. The word, however, can also be used for the activity leading up to the achievement of the seeing. Intellect will be systematically deceived if it thinks it is contemplating intelligibles that are in fact external to it. In sense-perception, direct contact *requires* externality because the composite physical object sensed must be other than the subject of cognition. See above 26–27. The sense faculty is identified only with the form of the sensible, but not its matter. See I.1.2, 26. So, the "truth," that is, the reality remains external. But since an intelligible has no matter, if that intelligible is "totally" (*malista*) external, what Intellect is identified with can only be a representation or simulacrum of it.

Above at 1, 1–2, Plotinus denies that Intellect can ever be "in error" (*pseusesthai*) and believe (*doxasein*) things that are not. The point here seems to be slightly different. One might concede that Intellect, since it has no beliefs at all, cannot believe the things that are not or be in error in this way. But even if it is granted that Intellect must cognize solely by contemplation, its objects cannot be external to it. Deception would then be possible even without false belief, though in a way it would be worse. For if one has false belief, it is possible that one should come to have a true belief about the same thing. If, though, intelligibles are external, Intellect could not possibly not be deceived in its false contemplation.

1, 54–58 *It will contemplate . . . and nothing true*: If the intelligible are external, then Intellect's cognition (*gnōsis*)—whatever it turns out to be—will not be knowledge. It can only possess reflected representations (*eidōla*) of reality. Such putative *eidōla* would be analogous to sensible forms in that they could not be the reality they reflect. The *disanalogy* between *eidōla* and sensible forms also needs to be stressed. The sensible forms are the forms of the sensibles and as such have intelligibility; the *eidōla* cannot be presumed to be such. For the *eidōlon* of a Form is not just that Form but is diminished in intelligibility. By having *eidōla*, Intellect will have only counterfeits of reality, fake diamonds, so to speak, rather than the real thing. The "falsities" (*ta pseudē*) are not, then, false propositions about reality.

1, 58–59 *If, then, it . . . share in truth*: If Intellect recognized that it has only counterfeits of reality and not reality itself, that would suggest that it could compare one with the other. Once, though, a comparison is made, Intellect could no longer take the falsities as true. In this it would be like one of the people in Plato's Cave who realizes that he has been systematically taking images (of images) as real. I take it that Plotinus does not regard this as a real possibility for Intellect.

1, 59–61 *But if it . . . from the truth*: The alternative—systematic and complete deception—is worse. Intellect would be like the "many" who in the Cave are unaware how far from reality they are.

1, 62–65 *This is the . . . what it has*: Plotinus now draws the conclusion that if having truth requires its internality to the knower, then there is no truth in acts of sense-perception, but only belief (*doxa*). That is, as a result of an act of sense-perception what the cognizer does come to possess is a belief. I take it that Plotinus includes in the "belief" both the "propositional attitude" and the content of the belief, some proposition or other. The belief must be different from that from which the belief arises, or from that which caused the belief, namely, the sensible object. At VI.9.3, 31–32, Plotinus says that belief "follows" (*hepomenēs*) the activity of sense-perception. These beliefs may be true in the sense that they have as objects true propositions, where "true" is a semantic property.

1, 63 *belief is receptive*: Plotinus says that "belief" (*doxa*) is "receptive" (*paradechomenē)*, deriving it from the verb *dekhomai*. The adjective *dochos*, meaning "containing" or "able to hold" suggests that the content of beliefs are "internal" to a subject but only in the sense that it belongs to them. So long as the belief is about that which is external, there is no ontological truth present.

1, 65–68 *If, then, there . . . truth to be*: If truth is not internal to Intellect because intelligibles are not, then Intellect will not be truth. But if this is so, then Intellect will not be real Intellect, which is to say that it will not be Intellect at all. The conclusion can be seen to be portentous, particularly if we set it within the requisite metaphysical context. Since all types of cognition have to be seen as hierarchically ordered and derived from their paradigm, it is not only the case that if Intellect did not exist, then no other rational cognition would be possible, but also no mode of cognition has the truth other than one that operates like Intellect. So, if we are to have truth, either we are intellects or we must somehow be able to "access" our intellects or Intellect itself. Plotinus' argument that the intelligibles are internal to Intellect is not only an argument regarding the possibility of intelligibility, but also the possibility of rational access to that which is intelligible. I think we may leave aside animal cognition which does not rise above imagination (*phantasia*), itself derived from sense-perception. Animals do not have intellects or access to Intellect, except in the sense that by receiving images of Forms, they have access to Intellect qua intelligibles.

Kühn (2009, 141–144) argues that in the concluding passage Plotinus' equivocation between truth as a property of being and truth as a property of propositions or thought makes invalid his argument for the conclusion that if truth is not in Intellect, then it is nowhere. See also Roloff (1970, 101). Kühn's objection confuses a relational property of being, truth, with being itself. As we have seen (*ad* l. 24), being is prior to knowing for Plotinus in the sense that the knower, Intellect, does not produce being by knowing. What Intellect does do, however, is make being to be known by its accomplished desire for the Good. The Idea of the Good provides truth to Forms, *Republic* 508e1, and knowability (*gignōskesthai*), 509b5. It is by Intellect that they are eternally known. Kühn is correct that this argument does not prove the internality of being; it proves only the internality of the intelligible, that is, truth, a property of being. But the property of being cannot be present without being itself being present. The presence of truth without being is, then, only the presence of semantic truth, that is, a belief with an intentional object, namely, a proposition, that has the property of representing being correctly or "of saying of what is that it is and of what is not that it is not."

The words "But there is nowhere else for truth to be" are intended to indicate that if the multiplicity of intelligible entities ("being") were external to Intellect, there could be no truth. That is, the internal relations among intelligibles necessary for the possibility of true propositions could not exist. See above on lines 49–50.

Chapter 2

Plotinus continues to derive the consequences of the internalization of intelligibles in Intellect.

2, 1–4 *One should not . . . eliminating Intellect itself*: If the intelligibles are external to Intellect, and only impressions are in it (see 1, 25 above), then Intellect is deprived of truth, ignorant of the intelligibles (*agnosia*), which are then rendered non-existent (*anuparxia*), and even Intellect is eliminated.

For Intellect, being deprived of truth is equivalent to the externality of intelligibles. This deprivation results in ignorance, not false belief, because Intellect would no longer be in contact with intelligibles and such contact is necessary for cognition of them. The non-existence of intelligibles follows from their not being known. And since Intellect's essence is to be a knower of all that is intelligible, it, too, would disappear. *Per impossibile,* if intelligibles were unknown, only the One would exist. A universe in which the One produced intelligibles or Forms alone without Intellect cognizing them is impossible. So, too, a universe in which the One produced Intellect and no intelligibles. Even though we need to argue for the internality of intelligibles to Intellect, we can infer the necessity for the existence of Intellect and intelligibles from their actual existence. Knowing that they do exist then, if they did not, the One would have failed to produce that which it could have produced. This is impossible owing to the diffusiveness of the One *qua* Good. See V.4.1, 34–36.

Plotinus frequently describes Intellect and the intelligibles that are internal to it as a "one-many." See IV.8.3,10; V.1.5, 18–19; V.3.15,11; V.4.1, 21; VI.2.2, 2; VI.2.10, 11; VI.5.6, 1–2; VI.7.8, 17–18, etc. What this means, among other things, is that Intellect provides the unity of the multiplicity of intelligibles, that is, the unity of being or *ousia.* Apart from their unity within the One itself, in which they are absolutely undistinguished, being would have no unity without Intellect. It is Intellect eternally thinking the intelligibles that enables them to be distinct yet one or unified. See V.3.15, 31–32. Cf. VI.9.1, 1ff. where Plotinus argues that unity is a property of being. Relying on Plato, *Republic* 509b5–7, where the Good provides the "to be" (*einai*) and the "essence" (*ousia*) to Forms, and *Parmenides* 142b7–8, where it is said that the *ousia* of that which is one is not identical with its *einai*, Plotinus maintains that each

Form or intelligible is complex: its *einai* and its *ousia*. But anything that is complex must be unified in some way if it is to exist or have being. The unity of the multiplicity of intelligibles is found virtually in the One and really, that is actually, in Intellect. In fact, the "to be" or *einai* of the intelligibles is the Intellect itself.

At VI.7.17, 35 Plotinus describes Intellect as "Form of Forms" (*eidos eidōn*). Cf. Aristotle, *On the Soul* (*De Anima)* 3.8.432a2. I take it that this is an expression that is equivalent to "one-many." The One must, therefore, be "without form" (*aneideon*) as it must be beyond a one-many.

2, 4–9 *But since one . . . to true Intellect*: "Bringing in (*eisagein*) knowledge and truth" seems somewhat vague. Accordingly, I take the following *kai*, l. 5, as epexegetic. So, (b) preserving real beings, and (a) knowing what each thing is explains in chiastic order what bringing in (a) knowledge and (b) truth means. Real beings must be preserved for there to be truth, that is, intelligibility, and knowing what each thing is, as opposed to knowing its properties, is the only thing that real knowledge is of. Presumably, the "qualities" (*poion ti*) is being used loosely here to refer to the commensurately universal properties of intelligibles since intelligibles have no accidental attributes. As Plato argues in *Euthyphro* 9c–11b, one cannot know the "property" (*pathos*) of a Form without first knowing the Form itself.

2, 6–7 *but not of . . . trace of reality*: See II.6.1, 43–44 and Plato, *7th Letter* 342e2–343a1, for the distinction between what the intelligible is in itself and its qualities or attributes. These are not accidental attributes, but properties that follow necessarily from the being of each Form.

Armstrong translates, "but not [only] the knowledge of each thing's qualities since [if we only had that] we should have an image and a trace of realities . . ." He thereby interprets Plotinus to be saying that Intellect's knowledge is to be comprehensive propositional knowledge, including all truths about the essence and properties of Forms. But if *gnōsis* here refers to the mode or cognition hitherto attributed to Intellect, this cannot be propositional knowledge. Knowing "what each thing is" cannot be cognition of a proposition expressing the essence of that thing. It must be in contact with the intelligible. Cognition of its properties is either not a matter of intellection but of some lower form of cognition or, insofar as Intellect can be said to have that, it has it only virtually, analogous to the way that the One is virtually all things.

2, 7 *reflected representation* (*eidōlon*) *and a trace* (*ichnos*) *of reality*: The term *eidōlon* has already been used for a "sense datum." See above 1, 18. The term *ichnos* perhaps recollects *Timaeus* 53b2 where the quasi-elements in the receptacle are said to possess *ichnē* of their own nature. In the context of that passage, these traces seem to be phenomenological qualities ("wetness," "coldness," "hardness," etc.) that can be taken to represent what cosmic elements possess, having been mathematically structured by the Demiurge. No Form has such phenomenological qualities, though Plotinus does think that Forms contain virtually the phenomenological qualities that will be evident when the Forms are instantiated in the sensible world. See IV.4.13, 3–7.

2, 7–8 *would not have . . . the things themselves*; *Not have* (*mē echontas*), *present with* (*sunontas*), *mixed with* (*sugkrathentas*): These are probably intended as synonymous expressions, hence the translation of *kai* as "or" instead of "and." All three expressions are ways of indicating the cognitional identity that Intellect has with intelligibles. Perhaps the shift from the singular in reference to Intellect to the plural in reference to human beings expresses the above possibility of cognition of qualities and our primary identity with our undescended intellects.

2, 9–12 *For in this . . . will be thinking*: These lines repeat the points made at 1, 4, 45, 67. Intellect is the "foundation" (*hedra*) for real beings. Plato, *Timaeus* 52b1, says that space (*chōra*) is the foundation for all things that come into being. The parallel between Intellect and space, identified by Plato with the receptacle, 50c–51b, and by Plotinus, following Aristotle, with matter, is interesting. Intellect is the foundation for reality; matter is a sort of non-being identified with the absence of any reality, that is, intelligibility at all. See II.4.16, 3–4. But without matter, nothing could come to be. See III.6.14, 1–2. In one sense, the opposite of matter is the Good or One. See I.8.7, 19–20. In another sense, the opposite of matter is Intellect, the foundation of reality or *ousia*.

2, 11–12 *they will be alive*: (*zēsetai*) and "they will be thinking" (*noēsei*). The subject could be Intellect or the "realities" (*onta*). Probably, Plotinus is referring to 1, 32–38 where the intelligibles have life and thinking in the sense that they are identical with that which has life and thinking, namely, Intellect. Ficino takes "truth" as the subject of "alive" and "thinking": *sed erit in ea veritas sedesque rerum, vivetque atque intelliget.*

2, 12–13 *All of this . . . and dignity be*: Cf. Aristotle, *Metaphysics* 12.9.1074b18, 21 on the "honor" and "dignity" of the Unmoved Mover, which Plotinus assumes is identical to Intellect and the Demiurge. The term "blessed" (*makarios*) is used to refer to the gods, at least as far back as Homer. The principal reason for blessedness is immortality. Perhaps Intellect is said to have "the most blessed nature" (*tēn makariōtatēn phusin*) because it, unlike we human beings, is never separated from its own immortal state. Cf. V.1.4, 16. The superlative blessedness and honor and dignity of Intellect does not mean that it is the first principle of all. These are properties of *ousia*, not of that which is beyond *ousia*.

2, 13–18 *Indeed, again, this . . . is this way*: See 1, 6–8. Nor has it need of the conviction (*pistis*) that would arise from a successful demonstration. Cf. V.8.7, 44.

2, 15 *self-evident* (*enargēs*): See comment on 1, 8. A self-evidential cognitive state is paradigmatically in Intellect. That is why no one could be more convinced of that which is self-evident than Intellect is. Since Intellect is identical with intelligibles, its cognition of them is self-cognition. The transparency of intelligibles to Intellect follows from their immateriality. Embodied intellects, such as human beings, can be in self-evident states, but the intentional objects of these states are not the really real. For example, it can be self-evident to one that one is having a headache. The intentional object here is not the headache, but oneself-in-a-headachy-state. That intentional object cannot be identical with the immaterial subject since it contains matter.

"Objectively," Intellect's self-evidence means that it could not be mistaken about the objects of its cognition. The fact that it is having a cognitional experience guarantees that it is in contact with the object of that experience. Because the experience is cognitional, that object is an intentional object. "Subjectively," the self-evidence is Intellect's awareness that it is thinking its own self, that it is intelligible. This subjectivity justifies calling its cognition an experience or *pathos*. Indeed, Intellect's life is this experience.

2, 15–16 *and if there . . . that is itself*: Intellect's awareness that it comes from the One is equivalent to its self-knowledge. It knows itself as a one-many and it desires the Good as object. Hence, it could not be unqualifiedly identical with that.

2, 17–18 *and because in . . . and really so*: The words *ekei touto kai ontōs* are quite compressed. The *touto* is vague, though it probably refers to the *ti met' ekeino* or "something" that comes after the One, namely, Intellect itself. In the whole passage, Plotinus is arguing that facts about the life of Intellect that we might infer from our understanding of its nature are self-evident to it without inference.

2, 18–20 *So, the real . . . what it expresses*: Truth in the primary sense is not found in some correspondence between the contents of Intellect's thinking and reality. I assume that this is what the metaphor of "being in harmony with" (*sumphōnousa*) conveys. What then is "being in harmony with itself"? Perhaps the harmony consists in the awareness by Intellect of the presence of intelligibles in it and the actual presence. Its self-awareness is thus reflexive, giving some sense to a harmonizing.

HS following Theiler adds the words "but what it expresses" (*all'ho legei*) in lines 19–20 to make the first clause parallel to the second. I translate this text. So, Intellect is what it expresses and expresses what it is. The expressing that Intellect does cannot refer to speaking or other verbal image-making. It probably indicates just the awareness that Intellect has of the content with which it is identical. One may compare the case of one "expressing" to oneself one's own bodily or mental state. Our expressions are always made with symbols of some sort, some sort of "mental language"; Intellect's must be otherwise.

2, 20–24 "Who, then, could . . . than the truth." A hypothetical refutation of Intellect's claim to knowledge would have to be based on a counterclaim that Intellect is deceived or not in harmony with the truth. But one could only make this claim if one were oneself in harmony with truth. In order to do this, one would have to be Intellect, for only Intellect is in harmony with truth, in the relevant sense, by being identical with it. Thus, *per impossibile,* the refutation would have to be "truer than truth."

2, 22 *you were to provide*: (*komisēi*). I follow Dufour in taking this as second-person singular aorist subjunctive middle rather than third-person singular aorist subjunctive active in order to agree with the second-person "you could not find" (*ou . . . heurois*) in line 24).

Chapter 3

Intellect is a great god, but prior to Intellect is a greater god, the One. All things depend on this god. Intellect is also the necessary intermediary between the One and Soul.

3, 1–2 *There is, then, . . . and the truth*: Intellect is identical with all real things, the intelligibles, or Forms, that is, the truth. Cf. V.9.6, 1–3. So, all (*panta*) real things are identical, but not in the way they exist virtually in the One. Intellect is here called one nature (*mia phusis*), emphasizing the paradoxical sounding claim that many things are one. Plotinus uses the term *phusis* for the One and for Soul along with Intellect. See II.9.1, 20. But Forms or intelligibles are also called "natures." See V.8.1, 34; VI.7.14, 16. The many natures that the Forms are are identical owing to Intellect thinking them simultaneously and also to Intellect being cognitively identical with them. That is, when it thinks them, it thinks itself. The "manyness" of the natures that Forms are is revealed in Soul and through the agency of Soul in producing the variety of things in nature. See V.9.6,

3–7. We can grasp that a bear is different from a squirrel and so that the Form of the one is a nature different from the Form of the other owing to our encounters with these embodied animals. This is not the way in which Intellect knows them. Intellect does not have at its disposal an encyclopedia of Animal Forms with pictures. It does not even have a table of mathematical formulae or recipes for making them. But it could not be true that bears are different from squirrels, though they are both mammals, unless Intellect was eternally cognitively identical with the Forms of these.

3, 2–3 *And if this . . . the universal god*: This is the first time Intellect is called a god in this treatise. But see V.8.13, 1. An individual god, however, has a specific nature. Since Intellect is identical with all natures, one could well think that it is a universal (*pas*) god. The multiplicity that this god is precludes its absolute primacy, even though not its universality. It is universal in the sense that it "rules" over everything possessing some measure of intelligibility. This includes everything in the universe except matter, which is utterly unintelligible. Only the One, whose causal power is unlimited, explains the existence of matter.

3, 3 *one might well think*: (*axioi*). A difficult word to translate here. The word might have been translated as "valorize." The other problem is the subject of this verb. Armstrong takes it as Intellect itself: "but it demands as of right that this which it is is universal god." Harder has "sondern sie [*mia phusis*, 3, 1] hat Anspruch darauf, der Gesamtgott zu sein." Dufour takes it as "cette nature": "elle se juge digne d'être toutes les réalités." It seems difficult to give this active verb a middle sense. In addition, it makes little sense to having Intellect making a value judgment about its own status. Certainly, there is no sense in which Intellect thinks that it needs to be elevated in the minds of persons below it.

3, 3–4 *And this nature . . . see the first*: Intellect is, unexpectedly, denominated "the second god" after its universal greatness has been indicated. Cf. V.8.9, 14, VI.2.22, 37 and below 4, 4 on Intellect as a "cosmic god" and an "intelligible cosmos." Intellect reveals itself in an odd way. Its existence is the conclusion of an abductive inference. Intellect must exist if there is to be truth in the world. If Intellect did not exist, the putative ontological truth would in fact be only what are images of reality. It is not the case that there would be another ontological truth, say, the physical universe. Without Intellect, the samenesses and differences we observe here below would not really exist. Intellect is revealed only as necessarily existing, not as something we experience. Even our own undescended intellects, with which we are identical, are "revealed" to us only as the necessary grounds for our cognitional lives. Thus, what our "seeing" (*horan*) the first god is supposed to amount to is obscure. Can we "see"—non-visually, of course—the first god directly or can we "see" only that it exists and is the source of all being? See Emilsson (2007, 207–213).

3, 4–6 *That first god . . . suspended from it*: The One is the first god, seated on a throne, with Intellect as a pedestal. Elsewhere, VI.6.9, 39–40, Plotinus employs the metaphors of "foundation" (*basis*), "root" (*riza*), and "spring" (*pēge*) in referring to the One. Intellect is "suspended from" (*exērtētai*) the One. This calls to mind Aristotle, *Metaphysics* 12.7.1072b14, where he says that the heaven and nature are suspended (*ērtētai*) from the first principle, which is the Unmoved Mover. The multiplicity or complexity of Intellect proves that it could not be the first principle of all. As Armstrong notes *ad loc.*, although Intellect is a pedestal for the One, the One is not supported or elevated by Intellect; rather, the pedestal is completely dependent on the One.

Why does Plotinus here add that the pedestal is beautiful? As he elsewhere asserts, beauty is identical with all the Forms. See I.6.9, 15 and V.8.9, 40–42. Plotinus is relying on *Republic* 517b7–c4 and *Timaeus* 28a2–b2 with 30d2. See the entire treatise V.8 titled "On the Intelligible Beauty." That beauty should be identical with all intelligible reality is a crucial feature of Plotinus' account of the ascent to the One. Beauty is also identified with the One, but only insofar as it is attractive to us. If we are going to encounter the One at all, it is through Intellect. In addition, because it is through Intellect that all intelligibility is furnished to the sensible world, our attraction to anything here below—whether sexual or otherwise—potentially sets us on the path to the first principle. The beauty that is Intellect or all the Forms is a central feature of Plotinus' interpretation of Plato's *Symposium* and *Phaedrus*.

3, 6–12 *For it had . . . even more honored*. Procession (*proodos*) from the One is necessarily in the direction away from perfect unity and so the product of procession must be inferior to the One. Both Soul and that which is soulless are obviously inferior in this way. But if there is something superior to Soul and inferior to the One its production would have to precede that of Soul. If it did not, then the One would have failed to produce something that it could have produced. This is impossible. We have already shown that Intellect must exist. The question remaining is whether Intellect is more or less inferior than Soul with respect to the One. Intellect is the closest possible hypostasis to the One because it is minimally complex or not-one. It is a one-many, as opposed to Soul which is a one and many. Soul is inferior to Intellect especially because it is temporal, having parts outside of parts. What is soulless perhaps refers to matter, which is completely without form and so without unity.

It must be emphasized that procession from the One does not diminish it in any way. This is also true for Intellect as it "processes" to Soul and Soul to nature. Thus, the metaphor of "emanation" has to be used with care. For example, when heat emanates from the sun, there is a loss of energy or mass. But the One is eternally diffusive and eternally complete or perfect.

The "indescribable beauty" is that of Intellect. Plotinus is here quoting *Republic* 509a6 where it is the indescribable beauty of the Good that is announced. Cf. V.8.3, 19; 8, 21. Because the One is virtually all that Intellect is, the properties of the latter can, with qualification, always be attributed to the former. Typically, Plotinus uses the word *hoion* ("in a way") to indicate the qualification. So, for example, the One has will (*boulēsis*) and *ousia* "in a way." See VI.8.13, 6–7. It is also, in a way, the *paradeigma* of all things. See VI.8.14, 39. It is Intellect that is the real or unqualified paradigm of all things; it is all things eminently. The One is all things only virtually, but in a way the paradigm as well. The order of the procession from lowest to highest is from the "viewpoint" of the spectators. This is also the order or the ascent (*anabasis*) for human beings from our embodied states to our true selves. This is, of course, the reverse of the metaphysical order of procession. Cf. I.6.9, 39–40 where the Good is said to be "the primary beauty" in a "loose manner of speaking" (*holoscherei logōi*).

3, 12–15 *After all these . . . preceded the king*: The pointed remark does not necessarily suggest that the spectators have seen that which immediately precedes the king. They may well have left much earlier.

3, 13 *suddenly* (*exaiphnēs*): Cf. Plato, *Symposium* 210e4, the culmination of the ascent to the Good.

3, 15–17 *So, this king . . . a foreign ruler*: The analogy between the king and the One fails with respect to the relation between the king and his subjects. Armstrong takes the first sentence to be pointing out that the king and his subjects are different persons. So, in the second sentence, he translates *allotriōn* ("foreign") as "different, alien people" in order to preserve the contrast. But if the One's rule is not over "foreigners," the contrast would still require that they be different, according to the sense of Armstrong's translation. In fact, as the next sentence shows, the point of the contrast is that while kings rule over foreigners (e.g., the contemporary "kings" of Egypt), the One's rule is over that which is naturally related to the One. Though the One is not related to anything (see VI.8.8, 12–15), everything is related to it as product to producer.

See above comment on 3, 6–12 for the One as being in a way the paradigm of all things and so naturally ruling.

3, 17–21 *rather he has . . . gods than Zeus*: The comparison now moves from kings to gods. Even though Zeus has a connaturality with the other gods, the One is more rightly called the father of the gods than is Zeus. Intellect is also called "father" by Plotinus, following Plato in *Timaeus* 41a7. See V.1.3, 21. All divinity in the intelligible world is more intimately related to the One than are the gods related to Zeus.

3, 19 *offspring* (*gennēmatos*): On Intellect as an offspring of the One see e.g., V.1.7, 39–41; VI.5.4, 19; VI.7.2, 48. The biological metaphor should be kept in mind in trying to grasp Plotinus' concept of emanation. The One produces everything naturally. The calculation that is both implicit and explicit in both Plato's and Plotinus' characterization of the activity of the Demiurge or Intellect does not belong to the One. Soul is indeed an "offspring" of Intellect (see V.1.3, 21) but this fact must be balanced by the fact that Intellect operates as an instrument of the One.

3, 21–24 *Zeus imitated him . . . existence of essence*: The Hesiodic comparison being made here is: Ouranos = the One; Kronos = Intellect; Zeus = Soul. Cf. V.1.7, 27–37. Elsewhere, Zeus can stand for the Demiurge (see IV.4.10,

1–4) or for the World Soul (see V.8.13). Zeus is not content with his own contemplation of Intellect, but looks to the external activity of the One which is just the "existence of essence" (*hupostasin ousias*), that is, the content of *Intellect's* contemplation. Cf. Plato, *Phaedrus* 248a, on the contemplation of Forms by the gods. At 246e4, Zeus is set at the head of this band of gods. On the distinction between "internal" and "external" activity (*energeia tēs ousias* and *energeia ek tēs ousias*) see esp. V.4.2, 27–33. Here there is a fairly clear assertion of the existentialist metaphysics of Plotinus. Of course, the One is also the cause of *ousia*, not merely the existence of it as Plato says about the Idea of the Good, *Republic* 509b6–7.

3, 22 *not holding himself to* (*ouk anaschomenos*): Armstrong translates "not satisfied with." *LSJ* gives no examples of *anaschomenos* meaning "satisfied with" not accompanied by the genitive. But if it means, as Solmsen suggests (1986, 69 and note 4), "not support" or "not bear" the contemplation of Intellect, then the text has Plotinus saying something quite inexplicable. So, Solmsen thinks we should not identify Zeus with Soul in this analogy. But this seems to raise more problems than it solves. A related problem is that there is no verb indicating what Zeus does given that he is not content with contemplating Intellect. MacKenna supplies "looks to" which is reasonable given the immediately preceding *theōrian*, but in this case it is far from clear what contemplating the One means beyond contemplating the contents of Intellect. Armstrong supplies "aspires to," which is certainly one way of taking "looks to." Harder has "nacheiferte." On this interpretation, Zeus aspires to emulate the productive activity of the One. As Soul, this would refer to the production of nature. Dufour supplies "*imita*" ("imitate") from *emimēsato* in 3, 20–21, which seems best.

Chapter 4

This chapter summarizes the argument of III.8. 9–11. It then distinguishes the One from any number.

4, 1–6 *It has been . . . not purely one*: On the ascent to that which is truly one see III.8.9, 4; III.8.10, 14–16, 20–23. On the inferior unity of Intellect see 8, 30–36; 11, 42. The allusion to III.8 is a crucial part of Harder's case (1936) that III.8, V.8, V.5, and II.9 were actually composed as one treatise by Plotinus. See Dufour (2006, Annexe 1, 399–406) for a summary of Harder's argument, and references to those who have either followed him or raised doubts about the conclusion. Dufour concludes that there is good reason to think that V.8. and V.5 comprise one treatise, but insufficient evidence for adding III.8 and II.9 as opposed to considering them independent works. In either case, it is clear that all four treatises were probably written close in time to each other and that they repeat common themes.

4, 1 *ascent* (*anagōgēn*): On the ascent to the One see III.8.10, 20; IV.9.4, 2; V.4.1, 2. The ascent is said to be to Intellect at V.7.1, 2. The goal of human life is in a broad sense unification or "becoming one out of many" as Plato says, *Republic* 443e1–2. Cf. *Phaedo* 83a7. See I.2.6, 17–18. The unification that consists in becoming a virtuous person ("personal integrity") is in the direction of the unification that is identification with one's undescended intellect. The ascent to "what is truly one" stresses that the unity of Intellect and the unification with it is not perfect. In the implicit conceptual space between unification with Intellect and unification with the One is to be found, if anywhere, the mystical dimension of Plotinus' thought. As Porphyry tells us (*VP* 23, 16–17), Plotinus achieved union with the One on four occasions. The last words of his VI.9.11, 51 "flight of the alone to the alone" (*phugē monou pros monon*) indicate the ideal, albeit without a clear idea of how this is done.

4, 2–4 "which, being many . . . one than it is many." Here we find the application of the general Platonic principle that x is f by partaking in Fness. As we have seen, everything other than the One is complex or many. Yet, all things are beings (*onta*) by being one. See VI.9.1.1; I.7.2, 1–6. In the latter passage, we have the important additional information that to the extent that things participate in oneness, they participate in the Good. So, everything other than the One must partake of oneness. A deep problem lurks beneath this seemingly straightforward line of reasoning. If things are one by partaking in the One, then, given that the One is, nevertheless, transcendent, it would seem that there must be a distinction *within* the One between that part or aspect of it that is participated in and that which is not. That is, the One must function like a Form. See Proclus, *In Timaeum* 2.313.15ff., who refers to Iamblichus as the first to see that a real distinction *within* a Form is required to solve the so-called Third Man Argument in Plato's *Parmenides*. But the One is absolutely simple. How, then, is it possible to participate in it without being identical with it? Conversely, how is it possible for the One to be more than or other than that aspect of it which is participated in? This problem is the source of considerable reflection among later Platonists regarding the correct characterization of the One and, indeed, the possibility of any characterization at all. The postulation of an absolutely unparticipatable and uncharacterizable "One beyond One" is an option taken up by several philosophers. Plotinus' solution seems to require him to say that things participate not directly in the One but only in images (*eidōla*) of it. See I.7.2, 5. This passage refers specifically to the way that soulless things participate in the Good, but the point is perhaps generalizable; its applicability to Intellect, however, is obscure since Intellect must be directly related to the One.

4, 3 *that which is not one by participation* (*to mē metochēi hen*) is slightly ambiguous. Armstrong has "the One . . . that is not one by participation," taking *to hen* as an implicit subject. Harder does the same thing: "das Eine . . . das nicht durch Teilhabe eines ist . . . " Dufour is more literal: "ce qui n'est pas un par participation." The latter is preferable since it retains the structure of abductive reasoning and does not leap to the conclusion that the One is being referred to. That there must be something that is one not by participation is a *reason* for positing the One in the first place.

4, 3–4 *not that which . . . one than many* (*mēde to ou mallon hen ē polla*): MacKenna has a most elegant, albeit loose, rendering of the entire line: "we need a unity independent of participation, not a combination in which multiplicity holds an equal place." Anything that is one by participation is multiple. Hence, only that which does not participate can be perfectly one. Whether that which is participated in *can* be perfectly one is, as indicated in the above comment, another issue. Something, e.g., Intellect, can be more one than many in comparison to Soul. But Intellect is still many. Although gradations of oneness are possible, anything other than the One is in a sense as much many as it is one owing to the fact that it and its *ousia* are really distinct in it.

4, 4–6 *and it has . . . not purely one*: The nearness (*egguterō*) of Intellect to the One results from its being its initial product, not of course from anything like spatial proximity. Cf. III.8.11, 42 where the word used is *plēsion*. That the One is "purely one" (*katharōs hen*) gives us the reason for claiming that the steps in personal integration or achieving unity are elements of purification. On philosophy as purification see Plato, *Phaedo* 65e6ff. Death, whether literal or figurative, is separation from the body and hence a kind of purification of "manyness." See VI.7.27, 19.

4, 4–5 *the intelligible universe, that is, the Intellect* (*ho men noētos kosmos kai ho nous*): See IV.7.10, 35 for the identification of Intellect as an "intelligible cosmos." Hence, the *kai* here is epexegetic. Cf. VI.2.22, 37.

4, 6–8 *Now we long . . . some way possible*: The longing for a vision of the One has to face the prospect that that which transcends *ousia* can in no way be an object of cognition. The sentence calls for a strategy for approaching the One which is either non-cognitional or which employs an alternative indirect method. Cf. *Timaeus* 52b2, where it is said that the receptacle or space is to be grasped not by the senses but by a "bastard sort of reasoning" (*logismōi tini nothōi*). Aristotle identifies the receptacle with matter and says that matter is knowable only by analogy. See *Physics* 1.7.191a7–8. In both passages, the problem is an absence of form. The One is not missing form, since it is missing nothing; it transcends form altogether. See VI.9.3 which elaborates on the point that it is not possible to speak or think of the One because it is formless.

4, 7 *not one owing to something else* (*ou kat' allo*): This picks up line 3. The One is not one by participation. Armstrong has "unrelated to anything else," though one would expect *pros* instead of *kata* if that were the meaning. See VI.8.8, 13 on the unrelatedness of the One to everything else. The intense longing (*pothoumen*) for union with the One is produced by the One itself. See VI.7.34, 1. The longing is, then, universal, and present even in those who do not recognize it. The longing to return to the One is as natural as its productive activity.

4, 8–10 *It is necessary, . . . the least bit*: The words "from this point" (*entautha*) refer to the stage in the ascent when we grasp the existence of Intellect as a one-many. See V.8.1, 1–6. The sentence is an exhortation to the student not to "backslide" and either stop at Intellect or to try to conceptualize the One as anything other than absolutely on.

4, 8 *rush towards* (*aixai*): A rare poetic term. See VI.7.16, 2; VI.8.19, 8; V.3.17, 17. See J. Dillon (1992, 133–134) on the possibility that Plotinus is here using language from the *Chaldean Oracles*.

4, 11 *If you don't . . . posterior to it*: If the One is made to be even minimally complex, then it will be two. But then the One will neither be identical with each "part" nor with the "whole." It would be that in which the "parts" and the "whole" would participate. See III.8.11, 12–15 and V.6. 6, 5–9 where the proposed "addition" to the One is thinking. In effect, what is here rejected is making the One into Intellect. The illicit duality would require a distinction between the One and its *ousia*. At Plato's *Parmenides* 142b7–8, this duality differentiates the subject of the second hypothesis from that of the first. Plotinus interprets this hypothesis as referring to Intellect and the first as referring to the One.

4, 12–15 *For it does . . . is among them*: Here Plotinus begins to address the question of whether the One is in any sense numerable, that is, whether it is a unit. See I.8.2, 5; VI.7.33, 16–21. In Greek mathematics, "one" is not taken to be a number because a number is defined as a plurality of units. Thus, "one" is a measure of number, not a number itself. Plotinus' point is more general. Consider a group of three. One is a measure of each unit in the group. But the group, the "whole" is also one, that is, it has a unity itself. The One is not reducible either to a unit or to the unity of such a whole. The One is, then, a measure, but not a measure in the sense in which a Form is. See below

4, 17ff. Cf. Alcinous, 163.14 Whittaker for the Platonic doctrine that a Form is a measure (*metron*).

4, 15–16 *If this were . . . prior to it*: If the One were taken either to be a unit or to be the unity of a whole, then that which would be the measure of both unities would be prior and *that* would be the One.

4, 17–18 *Not even the . . . quantitative number*: "Essential number" (*ousiōdēs arithmos*) and "quantitative number" (*ho arithmos tou posou*) are distinguished at VI.6.9, 34–35 and VI.6.16, 26 where the term for quantitative number is *monadikos arithmos*. Essential numbers are ideal numbers; quantitative numbers are participants in ideal numbers. Each of the groups of, say three, has a number of units equal to any other three. The ideal number Three would, then, not seem to possess units. Cf. Plato, *Republic* 529a2; *Epinomis* 990c6. According to Aristotle's testimony in *Metaphysics*, Plato identified the Idea of the Good with the One which produced the Indefinite Dyad and along with that then produced the ideal numbers. The Indefinite Dyad itself is *not* the ideal number Two, but rather the principle of multiplicities beginning with the ideal number Two. See V.4.2, 7–9; V.1.5, 4–9, 13–18; III.8.9, 1–5. In the first two passages, Plotinus seems to identify Intellect with the ideal number Two or Duality. But in the last passage, he distinguishes Intellect as a principle (*archē*) of number and as a number itself. The Indefinite Dyad is Intellect prior to its "reverting" to the One and becoming definite in multiplicity by contemplating all that the One is virtually. The sense in which Intellect is both an indefinite principle and a definite principle is articulated by Plotinus in terms of a distinction between potentiality and actuality. The primary justification for distinguishing Intellect as a principle of number and as a number, too, is that all essential numbers, insofar as they are Forms, are cognitively identical with Intellect. Thus, intellection is the principle of definite, essential numbers in that it is by thinking that they arise or have their being. The result of thinking is, first, duality, the essential duality of Intellect and the Forms.

4, 18–20 *For essential number . . . is a number*: The entire sentence is difficult. It reads: *ousiōdēs men ho to einai aei parechōn, tou de posou ho to poson met' allōn hē eti mē met' allōn, eiper arithmos touto.* Clearly there is here a differentiation of the functions of essential and quantitative numbers, though what this is exactly is elusive. Perhaps the contrast is this. Essential numbers, like all Forms, are always providing being to whatever is capable of receiving it. Quantitative number provides quantity "with other things" (*met' allōn*), that is, with continuous as opposed to discrete quantities. Thus, something with continuous magnitude can also have a number (e.g., it is one and divisible into some definite many). Quantitative number can provide quantity "even without other things" (*eti mē met' allōn*), that is, where there is no continuous magnitude, to the numbers used when we calculate, e.g., when I think that 4+3=7.

4, 20–24 *Since the nature . . . comes from it*: "prior numbers" (*proterois arithmois*) refers to essential numbers. Here Plotinus proposes an analogy: quantitative number is to essential number as essential number is to the One. The principle that governs the analogy is that the quantitative number and essential number are both imitations of what unifies them. Neither quantitative number nor essential number "uses up" (*analiskousa*) or "fragments" (*kermatizousa*) that which provides their unity. So, the One is not compromised in its unity by the fact that there are many ideal numbers participating in it and each ideal number is similarly not compromised by the existence of many iterations of quantitative number. That which unifies is a "monad" (*monas*) and that which is unified is a "duality" (*duas*). The duality refers to two (or more) units that are unified as the number two, and so on.

4, 24–27 *And the monad . . . not remain isolated*: See VI.6.14, 15–18. The familiar point that that which is participated in must be "over and above" the participant. The monad is not identical with either of the units in the number two, nor is it identical with the unity that number itself possesses.

4, 27 *though remaining what it is, it does not remain isolated* (*menousa ou menei*): MacKenna has "present without being inherent." All the mss read *ou menei*, but Beutler and Theiler, followed by HS_2, emends to *hou menei* ("where it remains"), which seems unnecessary. Presumably, the denial of "isolation" is equivalent to the affirmation of participation. Dufour has "elle est différente et, demeurant ce qu'elle est, elle ne demeure pas immobile." The word "isolated" is presumably what we are to understand from the fact that the monad does not remain. But perhaps, alternatively, we should understand "unconnected" or "separated." Clearly, Plotinus is trying to express in a paradoxical sounding way the quasi-relation of the monad to everything else.

4, 27–29 *How, then, are . . . in the duality*: Three questions about the unity of the duality are being posed: (1) how do we account for the difference between the two units of the duality? (2) how can the duality be a one? (3) is the one of the duality identical with either of the ones *in* the duality?

4, 29–31 *In fact, it . . . the same way*: "The primary (prōtēs) one" is the one relative to the participants. The participation in the one by the units of a duality is different from the participation by the duality itself. See VI.2.10, 3–4; VI.2.11, 11–12; VI.6.13, 18–25; VI.9.1, 4–6 on the various kinds of participation in unity. Cf. *SVF* 2.366–368 and 1013 for the threefold distinction among organic unities, non-organic contiguous unities, and non-contiguous unities.

4, 31–33 *A house is . . . one in quantity*: A house is one by having continuous parts related to a specific purpose. An army has the purpose without the continuous parts. See VI.6.13, 23–27. The house does not have the unity of the Form of House in which it participates because the Form does not have parts outside of parts whether continuous or not. The house is also not a quantitative one unless and until someone counts it as one. See VI.6.16, 12–26. At VI.2.11, 8–9, Plotinus appears to contradict himself when he says that a house (and a chorus and army and ship) are not one by continuity (*suneches*). He seems to be thinking of the continuity of an organic individual. There is in fact no contradiction. The term *suneches*, as Aristotle explains, can be used either for "contiguity" or "continuity." The former refers to parts that are physically touching or joined in some way but are distinct and the latter to parts that belong to an organic whole, that is, they are not parts when they are separated. See *On the Heavens (De Caelo)* 1.9. 278b17; *Physics* 5.3.227a10–b2; *Metaphysics* 11.12.1069a5–14.

4, 33–35 *So are the . . . the decad one?:* The question is whether the monads (*monades*) or units in a number are the same as the monad in another while the unity of one number is different from that of another.

4, 35–38 *In fact, if . . . is it here*: Plotinus' answer is that the monads or units are the same in a numbered group if any member of the group is taken as the unit for counting. Thus, if we are counting ships or armies or cities, if we abstract from the peculiarities of the members of the group, each can be taken as a monad or unit. If the units are the same for ships, cities, and armies, then they are the same for the units of five and ten. He assumes that the unity of each number is different, for essential numbers are not countable or addable.

4, 38 *If, then, there . . . them up later*: A reference to VI.6.5.

Chapter 5

A discussion of how the One is responsible for the unity, and the different kinds of unity, of all things.

5, 1–2 *But we should . . . come from it*: Here the One is referred to simply as "First" (*to prōton*). See VI.9.2–3 and where Plotinus explains further in what sense the One is first. At 3, 16 he speaks of "the Good or the First" (*to agathon kai to prōton*). The First remains "identical" (*to auto*) because even if other things "come from it" (*ginētai ex autou*), it is not dissipated or spread out in them. The term *to auto* is here being used in a technical sense, which should be kept clearly distinct from *homoion* ("same"). Only one thing can be identical; many things can be the same. It is precisely because many things can be the same, that Platonists argue that there must be something "over and above" them that is identical or, as we are inclined to say today, "self-identical." As we have already seen, only the One is unqualifiedly (self-) identical, for everything else is more or less a composite. See comment on 1, 36–37.

The problem Plotinus is here addressing is what it means to say that things "come from it" if it is in fact absolutely identical. Would not some "part" of it be separated from it, in which case its identity would be compromised?

The expression "from it" (*ex autou*) encapsulates the fundamental distinction made by Plotinus between the activity (*energeia*) "of the essence" (*tēs ousias*) and that which is "from the essence" (*ek tēs ousias*). See esp. V.1.6, 30–39; V.4.2, 27–33, etc. Intellect is identical with the latter; Soul is identical with the latter with respect to Intellect.

5, 1 *we should return* (*epaniteon*): See above 4, 12–13.

5, 2–4 *Then, with numbers . . . to that one*: Plotinus is here summarizing the distinction made above at 4, 33–38. The unit in a number is different from the unity that the number has. So, the essential number five provides the unity for a group of five which is distinct from the unity in any of the units of the group.

5, 4–5 *But in that . . . itself much more*: The priority of the One to "the things that have real being" (*tōn ontōn*) is greater than that of the essential number to numbered groups. The expression *ta onta* is typically used by Plotinus to refer to Forms and Intellect. He seldom uses the modifier *ontōs*, as Plato does, to distinguish "real beings" or "really real beings" from other things that are merely "beings."

The relatively greater priority of the One is difficult to grasp. I suggest that Plotinus is alluding to the fact that Forms do not participate in the One directly, for the One cannot be distinguished into that which is participated in and that which is not. See above comment on 4, 2–4. So, the unity that an essential number has does not result from participation in the One, at least not in the way that the unity that a numerable group has results from its participation in the essential number. The difference is a direct entailment from the fact that the One is not eminently anything, but only virtually all things. If the One were eminently anything, then it would preempt the role of Intellect. It, not Intellect, would be the locus of the paradigms of intelligibility.

5, 5–7 *And though it . . . generating real beings*: Someone might suppose that if the One "remains" (*menei*), then the production of real beings is attributable to something other than the One. Plotinus wants to insist that this is not the case. The use of the term "generating" (*gennēsai*) here is clearly metaphorical. Cf. V.1.6, 19ff.

5, 7–11 *And just as . . . sort of form*: Plotinus is here referring to quantitative numbers where the monad is participated in primarily or secondarily. Perhaps the primary participation is by a quantitative number in an essential number and the secondary participation is by an instance of a quantitative number. Thus, the number four participates primarily in fourness and two groups of four participate secondarily. This requires that we take *monas* to refer to an essential number rather than the unity of a quantitative number. But this seems supported by VI.6.4, 7.

Things that come after the First, that is, real beings, have something of it as "sort of form" (*hoion eidos*) in themselves. Since the One is beyond *ousia*, it can have no form. So, the possession of a form is not literal participation in it. By contrast, the participation of anything in its Form means that it is what the Form is eminently. Plotinus says it is a "sort of" form precisely because that in which it participates is not eminently that which the participant possesses. The One stands to Intellect, first, analogous to the way that form stands to matter, and second analogous to the way that Forms stand to their instances. The first analogy refers to the initial "generation" of Intellect prior to its turning back towards the One; the second analogy refers to Intellect when, in its desire for the One, it achieves this by thinking all that the One is virtually. See V.1.7 and below 5, 14–19.

5, 11–14 *And there the . . . of the One*: By participation in essential numbers, quantitative numbers exist; by participation in the One the essential numbers or essences or Forms in general exist. As we have already seen, the One is the cause of the being of everything. See above comment on 4, 2–4. In that case, in what sense are essential numbers the cause of the existence of quantitative numbers? The most direct answer to this question is that the intelligible world—Intellect and all the Forms—are the instrumental cause of the being of everything. See VI.7.42, 22; VI.9.1, 23. For example, we can, depending on the context, truly say that the ball broke the window or that the boy broke the window with the ball. There is no over-determination of causality here. The important difference in this analogy is that the One, unlike the boy, does not cause something to occur by moving itself. And as we have seen, the One is not eminently that which it causes to be and the essential numbers in this case are not virtually the quantitative numbers. There is no instrumentality in the production of Intellect and intelligibles because they are the first product, the "external" actuality of the One.

5, 14 *trace* (*ichnos*): See below 6, 17. Essence is a trace of the absolutely simple first principle of all, that whose "essence" is just its activities (*energeiai*). See VI.8.13, 7. The fact that essence or form is a trace of the One or the Good plays a central role in Plotinus' conception of beauty, identified as form. All types of beauty, because they have in them traces of the One, draw us to it.

5, 14–19 *And if someone . . . of all things*: Plotinus here begins to indulge in a bit of fanciful etymological analysis, borrowing from Plato, *Cratylus* 401c–d. See below 6, 1. That *einai* ("being") indicates *ousia* ("essence") is an important clue to Plotinus' basic metaphysical vocabulary. Since the One is "beyond *ousia*," it follows that the One should be "beyond *einai*"; otherwise, one would have to suppose it to have *ousia*, too. But the fact that the One is beyond *einai* does not mean that it is non-being or even non-existing. What it means is that the One is beyond the sort of *einai* that entails *ousia*. Stated otherwise, the only sense in which the One has *ousia* is that according to which it is absolutely identical with its *einai*.

5, 19–22 *In a way . . . insofar as possible*: Plotinus imagines that the fact that *einai* and *ousia* are as close as possible to the One is revealed in one who starts saying *hen* and ends the utterance with *on*. Deriving *einai* from *hen* and *on* is, of course, entirely fanciful.

5, 22–23 *Thus, that which . . . of the One*: Note that here *ousia* and *einai* are kept distinct. The imitation of the One is *ousia*. See above comment on 5, 7–11. Stated perhaps more precisely, the imitation of the One is *ousia* whose existence is really distinct from it. For the metaphor of "flowing" (*ruenta*) used to describe the One as producer see also V.3.12, 40 and V.2.1, 8, where we have *hupererruē* ("overflowing"). The flowing forth from the One or its diffusiveness does not generate a relation between the One and everything else because the flowing is eternal and everything is "contained" within the One, not separated from it. *Dunamis* is here translated as "power" instead of "virtuality" which would be barbarous English. But this "power" does not indicate any potency in the One and it does not, when exercised, establish a relation between two or more entities or substances.

5, 23–25 *And essence, looking . . . and "hearth"* (*hestia*): Armstrong, following HS_2 in their *apparatus*, and, apparently, MacKenna, has "[soul]" as the subject of this sentence, but that does not seem to be justified. HS_2 in the *Addenda ad Textum* in vol. 3 revert to *ousia* as subject. The subject could be *hē ousia kai to einai* or, as here, just *ousia*. The imitation is the utterance of the words *on, einai, ousia,* and *hestia*. Plotinus here follows Plato in the above-mentioned passage from *Cratylus*, where intelligible sounds are taken to imitate the reality they represent. So these words represent the One. The reason for supposing that "soul" is the subject is presumably the same reason for thinking that the subject of *axioi* at 3, 3 cannot be Intellect. See above comment *ad loc.* But since this passage is entirely metaphorical, making *ousia* or *ousia* and *to einai* the subject does not seem out of line. See Ferwerda (1982) who argues for an indefinite subject, a "someone" parallel to that which is suggested at 3, 3.

5, 26–28 *Thus, the sounds . . . of real being:* The generating in pain is, presumably, the production of the sound. This is analogous to the generation of being and essence, though there is, of course, nothing painful in that. We may suppose that the pain arises from an effort to emulate that which in principle cannot be emulated, namely, production of being and essence.

Chapter 6

Plotinus turns to deduce some of the entitative as opposed to the operational properties of the One. It must be beyond form or essence and, consequently, it is unknowable.

6, 1 *But let these . . . as one wishes*: Plotinus acknowledges the speculative nature of the etymologies in 5.

6, 1–5 *An essence that . . . necessarily without form*: Here we have a more or less explicit identification of *ousia* and *eidos*. The One generates Intellect, which is identical with all form. Hence, the form that is generated is not the form of a particular kind of thing, but of everything. See V.9.8, 3–4; VI.9.3, 4; V.1.4, 10–14; VI.7.17, 36; VI.7.32, 9; V.3.16, 28–33. The use of the lower case "f" here for form is not to suggest that Plotinus is not in fact talking about Plato's Forms. Rather, the association of *ousia* and *eidos* is general, and would hold, for instance for Aristotle, even if Platonic Forms are rejected.

The phrase *eidos ou tinos, alla pantos* ("form not of something but of everything") is ambiguous. If *pantos* means "all," then what the One generates is the form of each and every "something." So, to keep the contrast between *ou tinos* and *pantos*, we should perhaps understand "[form] of everything" to refer to Intellect in its initial generation prior to its thinking all form as a result of its achieving its desire for the One. The thinking of all form is the *energeia* of Intellect. See V.9.8, 15–17. When Intellect thinks all the forms, it does not thereby divide them; the dividing intellect belongs to embodied persons.

On the One being without form see VI.9.3, 4; VI.7.17, 36, 40; VI.7.32, 9. The principal consequence of the denial of form to the One is that, since form is a principle of limitation, the One is without limitation. If there were any limitation in the One's activity, this would have to be the result of the fact that the One is one sort of thing rather than another and as a result it has the limitations of the sort of thing that it is. The One, therefore, must be ultimately responsible for the existence or being of everything, including matter.

6, 5–6 *And being without . . . this is defined*: The association of *ousia* with definability has deep Platonic roots. See *Euthyphro* 6d9–e1 with 11a7 on a Form as *ousia* and therefore capable of definition. On the One as without "figure" (*schēma*) see *Parmenides* 137d8–e1. Aristotle says that *ousia* is a "this something" (*tode ti*) and it is perhaps this association or gloss that Plotinus has here in mind. See *Categories* 5.3b10: *pasa de ousia dokei tode ti sēmainein*; *Metaphysics* 3.6.1003a9.

6, 6–7 *But it is . . . was a "this":* It would seem that the reason why it is not possible to grasp the One as a "this" is simply that it is not a "this." The point being made, though, is slightly more subtle. If anyone tried to conceptualize the One as a "this" and therefore as definable, that which was putatively grasped could not be the One. For the One is the principle (*archē*) of all form and therefore cannot be that of which it is a principle. That is, a requirement for being the principle of all things is that the principle not be a thing or something definable. See III.8.10, 28–29.

The One is uniquely simple. Could we thus conceptualize the One? No, because that would mean supposing that its simplicity is a property or nature that it has, in which case there would need to be a real distinction between it and this property. But in that case, the One would not be absolutely simple.

6, 8–9 *But if all . . . the One is?*: The hypothetical questioner must here be taken to be assuming that all that is is a "this." So, Plotinus replies by asking which "this" among all the generated *ousiai* is the One to be identified with.

6, 9–11 *Since it is . . . is beyond being*: Plotinus infers that the One is "beyond being" (*epekeina ontos*) from the fact that it is beyond or other than beings (*ta onta*) and beings are equivalent to being (*to on*). See V.1.10, 2; III.9.9, 1; II.4.16, 25; I.3.5,7; IV.4.16, 27; VI.6.5, 37; VI.8.9, 27; VI.2.17, 22. Plato at *Republic* 509b9 actually says that the Good is "beyond essence" (*epekeina ousias*). Plotinus is justified in inferring that the One is beyond being because it is beyond *ousia* and *ousia* is either a "this" or all "thises" collectively. And it has just been shown that the One cannot be a "this." The metaphor "beyond" indicates here "absence of limitation or definiteness."

6, 11–15 *For "that which is beyond being" does not . . . this unlimited nature*: We might suppose that if the One is "that which is beyond being," then we thereby are referring to "that" as a particular kind of thing. Plotinus here insists that the phrase only implies (*pherei*) that the One is other than being, or beings, with *ousia*. Plotinus here employs a principle of "negative" theology with respect to the problem of how to refer to that which is not a "this." Nevertheless, the One has an "unlimited nature" (*apleton phusin*). The only other time Plotinus uses the word *apletos*, IV.8.6, 14, it qualifies the *dunamis* of the One. Clearly these are alternative ways of saying the identical thing, that is, the One's unlimited nature just is its unlimited power. There could be no unlimited nature with limited power nor unlimited power with a limited nature.

6, 12 *does not indicate its name* (*oude onoma autou legei*): Cf. Plato *Parmenides* 142a3.

6, 15–17 *Someone who wanted . . . of the One*: See above 5, 14 on the "trace" (*ichnos*) of the One. Someone who supposed that the One is a "this" is not only prevented from attaining to it, but even prevented from attaining to Intellect and intelligible being. See VI.9.4, 1–3 on how our "awareness" (*sunesis*) of the One is not by "intellection" (*noēsis*) but by something "greater than" (*kreittona*) that. Plotinus is here perhaps alluding to *Republic* 511b2–b2 where Plato claims that the knowledge of the Forms requires the ascent to the "unhypothetical principle of all" (*tou anupothetou tēn tou pantos archēn*). For Plotinus, that ascent would fail if this principle were taken to be a "this."

The argument may be this. Suppose that someone gave the One the most plausible name for a this, namely, "unity" or "oneness" and took that to be its *ousia*. If that were the case, then the One would immediately no longer be virtually all things; it would be an *ousia* among others. But if the One is not virtually all things, then the "trace" of it, Intellect, could not be grasped as the one-many it is. That is, one would be led to try to grasp the Forms each as separate and this, as we have seen, is impossible.

The reason for insisting that the proper cognitive orientation to the One is necessary even for intellection to occur may be found in the claim that the One is virtually all that is intelligible. So, one must grasp the virtual identity of all intelligibles, that is, the underlying identity of the various manifestations of being, for intellection to occur. The sort of identity Plotinus has in mind may be seen in mathematical and scientific equations. Evidently, to say that 3 = 3 is to say something different from 3 = 1+2. The latter expresses a type of identity different from the former and, of course, something more illuminating. The equation 3 = 1+2 implicitly claims, roughly, that "3" and "1+2" are two different ways of saying the identical thing. That "identical" thing is in one sense Intellect itself or being and in another sense, the One. Intellect is all that is intelligible because the intelligibles are not external to it and the One is virtually all that is intelligible.

6, 17–21 *But just as . . . the intelligible aside*: The attainment of the One's nature requires setting aside (*apheis*) the intelligible. See III.8.10, 31–32. We can learn that the One exists by an argument showing that Intellect is complex and that the complex is not self-explanatory. But learning the nature of the One requires a unique effort of abstraction. The contrast between knowing the existence of the One and its nature is not quite either Plato's contrast between knowing the *ousia* of something and its property (*poion ti*) or Aristotle's contrast between knowing the *hoti* of something or some fact and knowing the *di'hoti* or the explanation of that. The contrast is, though, in line with Plato's implicit distinction between knowing that Forms must exist and knowing their nature and Aristotle's implicit contrast between knowing that the Unmoved Mover must exist and knowing what its nature is.

6, 22–25 *The way it is . . . clear to ourselves*: Here Plotinus recognizes that the terminology or labels we use for the One are merely placeholders for the sake of our discourse. The inadequacy of naming the unnamable is a permanent feature of speech and thought. Reflection on this fact is increasingly thematized throughout the later history of Platonism in antiquity.

6, 26–28 *But perhaps the . . . negation of plurality*: As Plutarch, *De Iside* 381F, notes, Pythagoreans analyzed the name of Apollo as *a-pollōn*, that is, "without plurality or manyness." Plotinus' point is that the otherwise inappropriate use of names for the One might be mitigated if "One" were understood as indicating negatively that which the One is not, namely, "many" in any respect.

6, 28–30 *And if the . . . say that name*: Plotinus is perhaps here alluding to Plato's *Sophist* 244d, where the Eleatic Stranger argues against Parmenides that if the name "One" and that to which the name refers, namely, the One, are distinct, then there will be more than one thing in the universe, the One and its name. The point here is slightly different, though. If "One" is a name and also that which the name stands for, then it might be supposed, incorrectly, that this name (rather than another) is appropriate because it names something or a "this." See VI.7.38, 4–5, where it is denied that "Good" is the correct name for the Good.

6, 30–37 *For perhaps the . . . even know this*: The name "One" might be useful as a starting-point for the ascent to it, as opposed to the conclusion. If "One" is understood to negate all complexity, then the next step would be to realize that if the use of this name gives even the appearance of referring to a "this," then the name must be eliminated. The name "One" does not reveal a nature, something which someone might suppose to be the case if, like "Apollo," the name "One" were taken to be indicative of a "this."

The contrast between hearing and seeing is perhaps meant to indicate that sounds, when communicated, are always representational, whereas the One can be attained only by the direct contact of mental seeing.

Chapter 7

This section picks up the last point, arguing that intellection of the One is a kind of mental seeing.

7, 1–6 *So, again, since . . . along with it*: At *Republic* 507e, Socrates distinguishes between the object seen and the light, itself seen, by means of which the object is seen. Armstrong, following MacKenna, takes the words "by means of which" (*di' hou*) to be referring to light as the medium (*metaxu*) through which things can be seen. But as Armstrong himself points out, the claim that a light is a medium for sight is rejected by Plotinus at IV.5.1. In accord with the *Republic* passage, it seems better, along with Dufour, to take the light as that which illuminates the object rather than as a medium. Plotinus is evidently thinking along the line of the *Republic* analogy between the illumination of sensibles and the illumination of Forms by the Good. The latter is not the medium for intellection, but that which "illuminates" the Forms for Intellect. This illumination is perhaps to be understood as explained above (Commentary 6, 15–17).

7, 6–7 *For this reason . . . has been illuminated*: The analogy Plotinus is setting up is evident. Seeing the One is going to be like seeing the light that illuminates a sensible. But since the light illuminating the sensible is seen along with it (*sunorōmenon*), the task will be to abstract somehow from the sensible and just see the light.

7, 8–10 *But when there . . . to grasp it*: The beginning of this difficult sentence seems to be contradicted by the ending. Plotinus seems to be saying that the eye can see the light when there is no sensible object and then concludes that "even then" *(kaitoi kai tote)* the eye sees it as supported by something else. Presumably, this "something else" (*heterōi*) is the source of the illumination.

7, 8–9 *instant impression* (*athroai prosbolē*): Cf. III.8.9, 21 *epibolē athroai*.

7, 11–12 *For even the . . . that supported it*: This sentence, which seems pointless, is added for the sake of the next. If the light emanating from the sun were deprived of the mass of the sun from which it emanates, of course that light would be invisible because it would not exist.

7, 12 *supported* (*hupekeito*): I follow the correction of HS_2 in their *Addenda ad Textum* to the mss all of which have "on top of" (*epekeito*).

7, 12–16 *But if someone . . . not light alone*: The strained analogy is here concluded. If the sun were identical with its light, then this would be the appropriate analogue for the One in relation to Intellect. In that case, perhaps the light would be visible in itself, apart from the forms it illuminates.

7, 16–18 *The vision of . . . is in them*: The application of the analogy of illumination seems to be this: Intellect sees the Forms by the light that is identical with the One. It can only see the Forms insofar as the light is in them. See VI.7.16, 20–31 for the identical analogy. But in this passage the Good is explicitly said to be the "cause" (*aitios*) of *nous* and *ta onta* "by means of its own light" (*phōti tōi heautou*). Plotinus perhaps also has in mind *Republic* 511b5–6 where the assumption is that knowledge of Forms occurs when the Good is grasped.

7, 18 *since the light is in them* (*en ekeinois ontos horai*): With HS_2 I understand *ontos* as a genitive absolute referring to the light. Since the light is in the intelligibles, Intellect can see it.

7, 18–19 *But insofar as . . . sees it less*: The "inclination" (*neuousa*) of Intellect to the Forms must be hypothetical, since Intellect is eternal and immutable. To focus on the Forms would be to see the Good or One less owing to diminished attention. The hypothetical is relevant to the human embodied intellects in the above passage from *Republic*, where the "grasping" (*hapsamenos*) of the Good is followed by a descent "through Forms" (*di' autōn*). Perhaps the best way to understand the present line is to take it as referring to intellection generally, the paradigm of which, Intellect, is eternally seeing the Good in the Forms.

7, 19–21 *If it were . . . source of light*: Presumably, this "abandoning" (*aphēsei*) of the vision of the Forms and the subsequent seeing of the light and the source of light is another hypothetical. Again, the hypothetical would seem to be relevant to embodied intellects insofar as they are capable of setting aside intellection of Form for a vision of the One.

7, 21–31 *But since it . . . were not light*: Another extended analogy to vision. Plotinus has already shown that the objects of Intellect are not external to it. So, it cannot see anything that is external. It must see by a light that is internal to it. See V.8.10, 37. The Platonic theory of light that is being referenced here is found at *Timaeus* 45b–e. Plato held that fire, the source of light, actually has two sources, one external to those with vision and one internal. In daylight, the light emanating from internal fire coalesces with the light emanating from the external source. At night, the latter is extinguished, but there is still the power of the fire contained within the eyes and covered by the eyelids. Plotinus proposes that in darkness it is possible to see light in its purest form, that is, the light within the eye.

7, 31–35 *In this way . . . again, not internal*: The analogy to the vision of the One is now completed. According to my understanding of the entire passage and the general principles discussed above, the hypothetical nature of this analogy is resumed. An embodied human intellect will see the One when it realizes the unity that is virtually all that which is intelligible. The residual doubt—internal or not internal—is precisely what we should expect given what the One is. It seems reasonable to suppose that Plotinus is here trying to explain his personal experiences of the One that Porphyry recounts in his *Life*.

7, 34 *all of a sudden* (*exaiphnēs*): Cf. Plato, *Symposium* 210e4, where the vision of the Form of Beauty is said to occur "all of a sudden."

Chapter 8

Plotinus now turns to consider the omnipresence of the One.

8, 1–3 *In fact, one . . . does not appear*: The One does not come from or go anywhere because it is absolutely simple. But it *both* appears and does not appear. It does not appear because there is, again, no distinction within it that would make it possible for it to be distinct from the way it appears. Stated otherwise, the One is related to nothing. And yet it does appear. See VI.7.34, 8–9 where the One appears to Soul. It can appear because things can be related to it, as when they become aware of it through the technique discussed in the previous section.

8, 4 *preparing oneself* (*paraskeuasanta heauton*): As often in Plato, the term perhaps bears a religious connotation as in preparing for a ritual or revelation. Cf. VI.9.4, 26; VI.7.34, 10.

8, 3–7 *For this reason . . . with the eyes*: The "pursuit" of the One would be undermined by the fact that the One is not an entity that is other than the "pursuer." The meaning of "remaining in a tranquil state until it should appear" is glossed at VI.7.34, 8–12 as removing attachment to all form. At VI.9.4, Plotinus says that the One is always present to everything so that its appearance requires that the "contemplator" remove all obstacles to its appearance. Since knowledge is of form, preparation for the awareness of the One requires an ascent beyond knowledge. The reference to the "poets" is to Homer, *Iliad* 7.422.

The description of the goal of achieving a state of tranquility in preparation for a vision of the first principle can be usefully compared with the so-called Hesychast Movement in the Eastern Orthodox Church beginning in the 4th century. See Bradshaw (2004, 230–236) for a good account of the movement, whose principal effort was to "lead the intellect back to the heart" in order that the person can be open to receiving God.

8, 7–9 *But from where . . . which contemplates it*: The One is here compared to the sun. See Plato, *Republic* 508a–b. The "horizon" over which it appears will be Intellect.

8, 9–13 *For Intellect will . . . it nears it*: Both Armstrong and Dufour take "that which is beautiful" (*to kalon*) here to refer to the One itself. It is true that there are passages in which Plotinus refers to the One as the beautiful. See VI.7.33, 12–22 where the Good is identified with the "primary beautiful." But Plotinus also says that the One is "beyond beauty." I.6.9, 37–39; VI.9.4, 10–11; V.8.8, 5; V.8.13, 11–12; VI.7.42, 15–17. The passage from V.8 is particularly important, since as we have seen, the present treatise is probably continuous with that.

I am inclined to disagree with Armstrong and Dufour for the following reasons. First, as we have already seen, Plotinus identifies the beautiful with all the Forms (see Commentary 3, 4–6). Second, the word *ekei* ("the intelligible world") in the phrase "giving itself over to what is in the intelligible world" would on their reading refer to the One. There are occasions where Plotinus uses *ekei* to refer both to the One and to the intelligible world (e.g., I.6.9, 43), but nowhere, I believe, that the term is used to refer exclusively to the One. Armstrong awkwardly has, "giving itself up to him." Third, the entire paragraph is filling in the claims in the previous paragraph about the "process" of moving from cognition of form to something "beyond knowledge." Fourth, at line 13 the words "as it nears it" do not seem to make sense if Intellect is already contemplating the One.

The main obstacle to taking the reference here to the Forms is line 9 where the object of Intellect's contemplation seems to be the One. So, the apparent object of contemplation that "immobilizes" Intellect, the One, would seem to be identical with "that which is beautiful." But at V.8.8, 5–7, itself a difficult line, the One "presents itself to contemplation by being form" (*eis thean parelthon tōi eidos einai*). This line is consistent with the entire tenor of the present passage and those cited above to the effect that contemplation is a mode of cognition and that we must transcend that in order to have a kind of vision of the One. On my reading, "Intellect" is here, as in the last section, being used as a model for the ascent of embodied intellect to the One. There is in fact no ascent within the eternal. But consistent with his general "top-down" metaphysics, Plotinus will always explain the lower by the higher. Intellect's ascent from contemplating Forms to the experience of the One is actually our ascent. Given this, there is no need to take Intellect to be doing anything but contemplating Forms. Armstrong, in his note to this passage, seems to admit as much, saying that "[t]his passage is one of the most difficult in the *Enneads* to reconcile with the imposing descriptions of the changeless eternity of Intellect which we find elsewhere, notably in the first six chapters of the treatise *On Time and Eternity*, III.7. Plotinus here seems to be speaking directly from his own experience, without considering the metaphysical implications."

8, 13–16 *It did not . . . came to it*: The passage clearly sets out the consequence of the fact that the One is related to nothing. What appears to be its arrival is actually the result of the preparation of Intellect for it.

8, 16–21 *It is Intellect . . . at the One*: The One does not wait anywhere because it is nowhere. That is, there is nowhere specific that it is, implying that there is somewhere else where it is not. The One is omnipresent, but only in the sense that everything is in it. See VI.5.4 for an extended discussion of the omnipresence of the One. Also, III.9.4, 1; VI.4.3, 18; III.8.9, 25; VI.8.16, 6.

8, 20 *for it is not in place*: Intellect is not in place. See V.2.2, 19–20. Cf. VI.5.3, 1–5.

8, 21–22 *And yet it . . . and not two*: If Intellect were looking at the One and not at intelligibles, it would not really be looking but would be absolutely identical with the One. This is impossible so long as Intellect is regarded as eternally produced by the One. Thus, it seems that the sort of vision of the One, hypothesized here for Intellect, is not really other than a recognition by our embodied intellects of the fact that the One is virtually all things.

8, 22–23 *Now, however, because . . . is not Intellect*: At III.8.9 Plotinus has an extended discussion of how intellect attains the One. The crucial step in his reasoning is that the One is omnipresent, and so in us. That is, we can only have an experience of the One if we abstract from any consideration that entails that it is other than ourselves. As he says, for an intellect to see the One is for it "altogether to be not intellect" (*mē panta noun einai*, III.8.9,32) since when operating as intellect, we try to think things that are other than ourselves. We do have to go out of ourselves in order to access our true selves in our undescended intellects. But we have to go within ourselves to access the One. Cf. V.1.10–11 on how the One (and Intellect and Soul) are found within ourselves.

8, 23–27 *It is wondrous . . . marvel at it*: For someone who understands that the One is virtually all things, its presence cannot be alongside or other than that to which it is present. Its omnipresence, if taken as a revelation, is falsely conceived.

8, 27 *And this is how it is*: This awkward transition is owing to Ficino's division of the sections.

Chapter 9

The discussion of the omnipresence of the One is continued and the hierarchical nature of reality is considered in the light of this.

9, 1–2 *Everything that comes . . . which made it*: The general principle that everything that comes to be is in another is enunciated at II.9.1, 10–11. The last clause of the sentence, "supposing there were . . . which made it" seems to refer to the possibility of an intermediary cause. Thus, Intellect is in the One and Soul is in the One by means of Intellect. The use of "in" (*en*) to indicate causal dependence is borrowed from Aristotle. See *Categories* 2.1a24 where Aristotle says that accidents are in a substance but not as parts. That which is in the One is, however, not in it as an accident, since the One is not a substance. Here, "in" indicates the existential dependence of everything on the first principle.

There is a slight ambiguity in this sentence. The alternative presented "either in that which has made it or in something else" might be read to indicate that if, say, Intellect is an intermediate between the One and Soul, then not only is Soul in Intellect, but in this case Intellect made it (*pepoiēkoti*), not the One. I do not think this can be right, since the One is the cause of being of everything, including all that is caused to be with the instrumentality of Intellect, and then with the instrumentality of Intellect and Soul (see Commentary 4, 2–4). The instrumental causality of Intellect is discussed above in the comm. on 5, 11–14.

9, 3–4 *For since that . . . is in another*: The point is that the sustaining cause must also be the originating cause. See VI.2.11, 26–29 for the distinction. The point would be more perspicuous if it were a case of that which is in time, that is, has a beginning, a middle, and an end. But it is also true for that which is not in time. See II.4.5, 25–28; II.9.3, 11–14. The term "everywhere" (*pantachou*) is evidently being used metaphorically to refer to every part of the generation, as if Intellect were produced in time. Intellect is "in another" because the One sustains its existence always. The reference in HS_2 to *Parmenides* 145b6–7 does not appear correct.

9, 5–7 *So, things which . . . which is first*: The metaphysical "nesting" here has the logical conclusion that everything is "in" the One. But of course this does not compromise the

One's absolute simplicity. It does, however, make evident its omnipresence.

9, 7–10 *But since the . . . prior to themselves*: The metaphor indicating that the One "encompasses" (*perieilēphe*) all is the correlate of the metaphorical use of "in" 9, 1–2.

9, 10–11 *Encompassing them, it . . . held by them*: Cf. III.8.10, 10–11 which compares the One to the root of a plant whose power is spread throughout the plant without it being separated from itself.

9, 11–13 *In holding them . . . is not there*: This ubiquity of the One is inferred from its being the cause of the being of everything. If the One were absent anywhere, that would mean it was not the sustaining cause of what is there. In that case, there would in fact be nothing there.

9, 13–15 *So, it is . . . from being anywhere*: To be somewhere is to be dependent on the One. Since the One is not dependent on anything, it is nowhere; since everything is dependent on it, it is everywhere. The One is able to be everywhere because it is beyond *ousia*.

9, 15–18 *For, again, if . . . things after it*: The possibility of the One being limited by another would require that the One not be the other, that is, that it be different from it. In that case, the One could not extend its causal reach beyond that which prevented it from doing so. If something prevents the One from doing anything, then the One is dominated by it to that extent. For example, if Intellect prevented the One from being the originating or sustaining cause of the being of Soul, this would happen because there was some incapacity of the One in relation to Intellect. That is, something the One is or has prevented it from going beyond Intellect. But there can be no such thing since the One is beyond *ousia*.

9, 18 *The things which . . . they are not*: If this is a reference to things that are contained in or parts of a whole, then the whole is only present where the part is in the sense that it is present where all the parts are together. I do not understand Armstrong's translation "[t]he things, therefore, which are in something are there where they are" taking the subject of the verb "is" to refer to the plural "things" contained, and not to the singular "container" (see Commentary 9, 18–21).

9, 18–21 *But as for . . . it is nowhere*: The One, by contrast, though it "contains" in a sense, does not contain in the way that entails that the container is present where the contained is. See Plato, *Parmenides* 138b5–6.

9, 21–22 *If, then, it . . . separate from anything*: Because the One is nowhere, there is nowhere that it is not. The point is that if it is everywhere, then it is somewhere; if it is somewhere, one might suppose, falsely, that there is somewhere that it is not. See Plato, *Parmenides* 144b2.

9, 22–26 *And if it . . . held by it*: That the One is "self-contained" (*eph' heautou*) is said to emphasize that its omnipresence does not compromise its absolute simplicity. Cf. V.4. 2, 13; VI.9.6, 15; V.1.10, 7–11.

9, 26–29 *Consider the cosmos . . . are in it*: The reference appears to be to the sensible cosmos, not the sensible cosmos plus the intelligible realm. At VI.4.2, 3, Plotinus distinguishes the "true totality" (*to alēthinon pan*), that is, the intelligible realm, from the "imitation" (*mimēma*) of it, "visible nature" (*horatē phusis*). There is no visible cosmos prior to the sensible cosmos. For this reason, the visible cosmos is not in place. The "cosmos" (*kosmos*), alternatively called "the all" (*to pan*), is normally used by Plotinus for the "container" of everything sensible. See IV.8.2, 14–19; VI.5.10, 36–39; II.9.17, 54; II.1.1, 12–16; II.3.16, 45–46.

9, 29–32 *And Soul is . . . else* [*the One*]: The cosmos is in Soul and not Soul in the cosmos, as Plato maintains. Here Plotinus seems not to distinguish the soul of the cosmos from the hypostasis Soul. See IV.3.22, 8–11, referring to *Timaeus* 36d9–e3. This is said despite the fact that at 34b the Demiurge puts the soul of the cosmos into the center of the body and then has it spread out throughout the cosmos to the periphery and beyond. In addition, the parts of the human soul are located in different places in the human body. See 44d–45b and 69d–72d. From the fact that everything is in the One, it would follow that Soul and Intellect are in the One, which is everywhere but nowhere. But it does not seem to follow that the body of the cosmos is therefore in its soul. One would have to add the premise that if Soul is in Intellect and Intellect is in the One, then Soul cannot be in anything other than that which is above it or that which contains it. Then, the relation between soul and body is governed by the relation between Soul, Intellect, and the One.

9, 32–33 *And there is . . . are in it*: The first principle of all cannot be in anything. Therefore, it is nowhere. This means not that it is not present anywhere, but that everything is in it.

9, 34–35 *Therefore, it is . . . it holds everything*: It is the nature of something with *ousia* to be cut off from things that it is not. Thus, it is possible for it to have external relations to other things. Since the One is beyond *ousia*, it is related to nothing. The containment of all things by the One does not put it into relation with all things, but rather they stand in relation to it. The containment is equivalent to total existential dependence.

9, 36–38 *For this reason . . . being than others*: Everything depends on the One for its existence. And for this reason, it is the Good of all things. See VI.2.11, 26. Since everything that exists exists as a certain kind of thing, each thing depends on the One in a different way. This opens up the possibility of graded participation in the One. One thing is better than another and therefore closer to the One because it has more being (*mallon on*) than another. Although the One is above the being of anything with *ousia*, it is the standard for gradation of being because everything strives to achieve unity or integrity according to its nature. The greater is the unity, the closer to the One.

The inference from "everything depends on the One" to "the One is the Good for everything" seems immediately obvious to Plotinus, though one might raise the question of its cogency. Why is it not possible that something's good should be found in that which is other than that which produced it or caused it to be? The answer is that the good of anything consists in fulfilling its own nature, a nature that is found paradigmatically in Intellect. So, everything aims to become "one out of many," that is, to become ideally what it is. The One is the Good for everything because it is virtually what all these paradigms are. Only creatures with intellects, however, are able to have some sort of cognitive awareness of the One beyond Intellect.

9, 37 *better* (*agathōtera*): This is an extremely rare use of the comparative *agathōteros* by Plotinus. The only other passage is VI.6.18, 21. Perhaps he wishes to preserve the root *agatho-* in reference to the Good or One.

Chapter 10

The necessity for grasping the One without intermediaries. The problem of a "part" grasping a "whole."

10, 1 *But please do . . . through other things*: At III.8.10, 34–35, Plotinus urges his readers to see "the greatness of [the One] by the things that come after it and through it" (*sunorōn de to mega autou tois met' auto di' auto ousin*). If this passage is not to contradict the present one, then we need to lay emphasis on the mediation of "things that come after it" for seeing the greatness of the One, not the One itself. Its greatness consists in the fact that it is virtually all things. Setting aside "other things" is evidently necessary for direct awareness of the One. Note the informality of the second person singular, referring perhaps to any of the members of his seminar. See VI.7.35, 33–36, where the terms "confounding" (*sugcheasa*) and "effacing" (*aphanisasa*) are used to indicate how the soul surpasses Intellect or perhaps bypasses its own intellect. The metaphors suggest that it is the multiplicity of intelligible objects that needs to be overcome in seeing the One.

10, 1–2 *If you do . . . it, not it*: For Intellect as a "trace" (*ichnos*) see above (Commentary 5, 14).

10, 2–4 *But think what . . . nothing holding it*: See above chapters 4 and 9 on the initial use of the metaphors in this sentence.

10, 4–5 *For there is . . . of this sort*: That which must exist is an absolutely simple first principle of all. Its necessary uniqueness follows from its simplicity. From both its uniqueness and simplicity follows the impossibility of grasping it. The words "something of this sort" (*ti toiouton*) do not imply that the One has an *ousia*. They indicate only that there must exist a first principle of all.

10, 5–7 *Who, then, could . . . differ from it?:* A new point. Since the One is all things, grasping it would require a grasp of that which is grasping it. The irreducible duality of cognition makes grasping the One impossible.

10, 7–8 *Does one, then, . . . as a whole*: The goal is to experience the One, which is all things, but it cannot be described in its totality. The adverb "comprehensively" (*athroōs*) indicates the resolve of someone to experience that which is all things "all at once" with the attendant difficulty of doing this.

10, 8–10 *Otherwise, you will . . . at the whole*: That the experience of the One transcends intellection is here made explicit. See III.8.9, 21–22 where transcending intellect involves a "comprehensive intuition" (*epibolēi athroai*) of the whole, but not a whole of parts. Cf. VI.7.35, 21–22.

10, 10–15 *And when you . . . all things come*: Now the seeker reverts to thinking of the One. First, he identifies it as the Good. On the Good as virtually all things (see Commentary on 1, 41–43). Because the Good is virtually all things, it is the cause (*aitios*) or explanation for all things.

Plotinus here imagines an experience of the One, followed by an attempt to remember that experience. The attempt to remember the One, since this experience is unique, reverts to an attempt to conceptualize it, which is impossible. Cf. V.1.1, 1ff. on the "forgetting" by souls of their father. The theme of memory is an important one for Plotinus. See IV.3.24 – IV.4.12 for the most complete discussion. We can only remember what we have experienced. Even if we could remember a previous experience of union with the One (as Plotinus himself presumably could) that would not amount to remembering the One as if it had properties we could recollect. See also VI.9.11, 43–45. The forgetting and remembering of the One leads to the exhortation to recover our true identity, not of our previous experiences. This identity could never be recovered by a technique of the recollection of previous experiences.

That the Good is the One, Plotinus takes from Aristotle's testimony and from his reading of *Parmenides.* That it is the "principle of all" refers to Plato, *Republic* 511b7. A true principle of all must be "simple and first." Cf. II.9.1, 1–2.

10, 12 HS_2 in their apparatus refer to *Republic* 521a4, which appears to be an error. The comprehensive grasp of the Idea of the Good, represented as the sun at *Republic* 516b4–7 is perhaps the passage Plotinus has in mind.

10, 15–19 *The first motion . . . it is first*: The first motion will be the motion of Intellect. See V.1. 6–7. Also, cf. VI.2.7. See Plato, *Sophist* 254d5. The denial of motion and rest to the One is taken from *Parmenides* 138d4–5 and 139a3–4.

10, 19 *But it has . . . it be so?*: See Plato, *Parmenides* 137d7.

10, 20–21 *And yet it . . . need of anything?*: Cf. Aristotle, *Metaphysics* 12.7.1073a8–11 on the Unmoved Mover being neither finite nor infinite in magnitude. Whereas unlimitedness is usually taken as a defect, since it is the contrary of form, the fact that the One is not unlimited in magnitude is not a defect in it. See VI.5.4, 13–15.

10, 21–23 *No, it is . . . lacking as well*: See VI.9.6, 10–11. The unlimitedness of the One means that Intellect and Soul, insofar as they are relatively unlimited, will not have defects. See III.7. 5, 23–24. Also VI.4.2, 14–15; VI.4.5, 3–6; VI.4.8, 25–28; VI.4.11, 3–6; VI.5.4, 15; VI.5.9, 19–20.

Chapter 11

The reality of the immaterial and the association of the immaterial with divinity.

11, 1–2 *Further, this is . . . have a limit*: If the first principle were, *per impossibile*, more than one, then it would be the product of the One and the Indefinite Dyad, and therefore it would be limited. The last clause "it has nothing in relation to which something that comes from it will have a limit" (*mēde echein pros ho horiei ti tōn heautou*) is difficult. The sense seems to be that because the One is unlimited, it cannot be the source of limitation in anything that comes from the One. So, all the limitations flow from *ousia* in Intellect, and from Soul as a principle of desire. Thus, in any composite, the One by causing that thing to exist is a principle of unlimitedness for that thing, but not the unlimitedness of matter. Cf. V.8.9, 24–25 on the unlimited power of the One.

Plotinus here seems to reject the theories found within the Platonic tradition according to which the One imposes limit on the Indefinite Dyad, thereby producing the Forms or Numbers. But the One could not be a principle of limitation. The One produces the Indefinite Dyad, which is just Intellect in its logically first phase. Limitation is produced then by Intellect itself when it turns to the One. Cf. VI.7.17, 14–16. The denial of the One as a principle of limit follows from Plotinus' rejection of dualism of any sort, especially that which makes the Indefinite Dyad an irreducibly first principle of unlimitedness, thereby requiring the One to be a coordinate principle of limit.

11, 2–3 *For by being . . . amount to a number*: On the One as being measure and not measured, see above 4, 13–14. On the One not being a number see above 5, 2–4. There is no number one in any case, since a number is a plurality of units. But the One could not even be a unit for counting numbers since it is neither a magnitude nor is it a discrete quantity.

11, 3–4 *It is not . . . would be two*: The One has no relation to anything else (see Commentary 5, 22–23). If the One were related to itself, there would have to be within it a distinction between the "parts" that are related. But this is impossible.

11, 4–5 *Nor does it . . . have a shape*: On “figure” see Plato, *Parmenides* 138d1; on “parts” see 137d2–3, 138a1.

11, 5–8 *Do not seek . . . things are sensible*: The contrast between perceptual seeing and intellectual seeing is a fundamental distinction within Platonism. There are many terms drawn from the perceptual vocabulary, like *theōrein*, that are used metaphorically for an act of intellect.

11, 7 HS_2, following a suggestion of Igal, inserts <*ha*> (“that”) between *aisthēta* and *einai*, on the grounds that a relative pronoun is required for the participle *hupolambanōn* (“supposing”). It is difficult to construe the sentence without some such addition. Cf. the *ha* in line 8 which seems to be in contrast to a *ha* in line 7.

11, 8 *By supposing that . . . exists most of all*: What is the criterion by which we can say that one thing exists more than another? In the present context, it is presumably unlimitedness.

11, 8–10 *For those things . . . less of it*: These are sensibles. See V.9.1, 3–4; III.6.6, 65–69. Plato’s Allegory of the Cave at the beginning of Book 7, 514aff. of *Republic,* presents us with the radical conversion experience of someone who comes to “see” that what he had hitherto thought was most real is actually most unreal and that of which he was totally ignorant is the most real of all.

11, 10–11 *That which is . . . first than essence*: The priority of the One to essence is a reference to that priority as expressed by Plato, *Republic* 509b9, of the Idea of the Good to the intelligible world. On the One as the "principle of being" where "being" refers to Intellect and intelligibles see V.9. 5, 26; V.9.6, 1–2; V.9.8, 16–17. The "principle of being" qua principle does not have being, where "being" refers to the existence of something with an essence or form. It has or is unlimited being.

11, 11–16 *So, you should . . . the rites within*: Evidently a reference to Plato, *Phaedo* 81e5, where the mention of gluttony is in the context of a discussion of reincarnation and the fate of one who was a glutton in a previous life. Cf. *Timaeus* 73c6–8 and *Phaedrus* 238b1.

11, 16–22 *For in these . . . back to sleep*: The contrast between what we see when awake and what we dream when asleep is a commonplace in the Platonic tradition for representing the difference between the intelligible and the sensible realms. Cf. Plato, *Republic* 533b, 534c.

Chapter 12

The priority of the Good to the Beautiful.

12, 1–5 *It is necessary . . . were not seen*: The word "each" refers to sensibles and intelligibles. The former are cognized with the five senses; the latter are cognized with the intellect alone. Cf. Aristotle, *On the Soul* (*De Anima*) 3.3–4, where Aristotle, discussing his predecessors who held that thinking is a sort of sensing, argues that, though there are similarities in the two cognitive functions, there are fundamental differences, too.

12, 5–7 *It is necessary . . . for and desire*: Cf. V.1.1, 1–2, where Plotinus explains the human fall into embodiment as resulting in a "forgetting" (*epilathesthai*) of their father, god. That which people originally desire is the enjoyment of the Good. This is a desire that is eternally fulfilled in Intellect and in the undescended intellects of human beings. See above (Commentary 10, 10–15) on the cognitive challenges involved in attaining to the One. Here,

Plotinus focuses on a strategy relying on the affective dimension of embodied life. Our desire for the Good is a permanent fixture of our nature. The beautiful is how the Good appears as attractive.

12, 7–9 *For all things . . . able to exist*: The necessary desire for the Good is the obverse of its necessary production. See VI.5.1, 11–13; V.6.5, 18–19; I.7.1, 9–13 on the desire of all things for the Good. Cf. Plato, *Republic* 505d11–e2. See above (Commentary 9, 36–38) on the need to distinguish between the following two claims: (1) all things exist owing to the One, and (2) all things desire the Good because they owe their existence to it. The former is argued for by Plotinus in various places. The latter claim is different, and perhaps not obviously a consequence of the former. The two claims are to be understood as mutually entailing when we add that Good = One. It is not possible not to desire the creator and sustainer of all things if all things desire the Good and the creator and sustainer is just that. Desiring the Good should be expanded into "desiring to possess the Good" where possession consists in cognizing all that the Good (= One) is virtually.

12, 9–11 *And the apprehension . . . awakening of love*: Plotinus here begins to contrast the desire for the beautiful with the desire for the Good. See above (Commentary 3, 4–6) for the identification of the beautiful with all the Forms. The argument from recollection in Plato, *Phaedo* 72e3–78b3 shows that we know Forms prior to embodiment, even though we have forgotten them. Hence, we know them "in a way." In *Phaedrus* 249dff., Socrates describes the madness of the lover who sees embodied beauty and is reminded of the intelligible beauty he had experienced prior to embodiment.

12, 11–13 *But the Good . . . recollection of it*: Compared with Forms, the Good is in a way at once more and less remote to us. It can never be, like Forms, recollected. But it is even more intimately present to us than the Forms prior to their being recollected. Since all things are contained within the Good, and the Good is virtually all things, our awareness of it is just our awareness of our own existence. The Good is present to us even when asleep, that is, even when we are not aware of its presence.

12, 13–14 *People do not . . . they are asleep*: This line essentially repeats line 12, but for the addition of "because" (*hoti*). Perhaps Plotinus' point is that since the Good is present when we are asleep as well as when we are awake, we do not notice any difference and so we do not notice it when awake.

12, 14–15 *But the love . . . having seen it*: See Plato, *Phaedrus* 251c–e; *Symposium* 206c–e. The love of the beautiful is just the desire for the Good. See Plato, *Symposium* 204d–e. So, seeing something beautiful, the "necessity of nature" as above, compels one to pursue it.

12, 15–17 *This love is . . . to be secondary*: Since the Forms are derived from the Good, the love of them is secondary, meaning that love of the Good is manifestly in love of knowledge of Forms. An additional indication that the love is secondary is that we can be conscious (*sunientōn*) of this. The point is, I take it, that we can only be conscious of that which we cognize. This requires a differentiation of subject and object. The fact that we can be conscious of beauty shows that beauty is not the primary Good or object of desire.

12, 17–19 *But the desire . . . ancient and prior*: The priority of the Good to the beautiful, that is, to all intelligibles, is here clearly stated. Cf. I.6.9, 37–43. Previously, at 7, 1ff., it is said that the Good is beautiful. This designation is of a piece with all the positive attributes of the Good or One, namely that it is or has these attributes "in a way" (*hoion*), that is, it has them as a cause contains its effects. And in the case of the Good, it is their cause in the sense that it is virtually all of them.

See Edwards (1991) on some of the Middle Platonic treatments of the Good in relation to that which is beautiful.

See esp. Alcinous, *Didaskalikos* 165.27–31 Whittaker. Edwards, rightly in my view, rejects Armstrong's claim that in subordinating the beauty of the Forms to the Good, Plotinus is deviating from Plato.

12, 19–24 *Everyone thinks that . . . which is good*: The argument here is very compressed. Plotinus is referring here to Plato, *Republic* 505d5–e1, where Socrates says that while people are satisfied with the apparently just or beautiful, they are not satisfied with the apparently good. So, the good at which people aim is always the real good. If someone attains what he thinks is good, he assumes that this is the real good and not merely the apparently good. The contrast "beautiful in itself rather than beautiful for them" in intended to provide a comment on the previous sentence. Since people want the real good—whether or not they actually possess it—when they possess something they think is good, they are content. They think they actually possess the real good. But since people are content with the apparently beautiful, they think that the really beautiful is not something they possess, but something that is apart from or outside themselves.

12, 24–30 *For they argue . . . comes before him*: The point seems to be that, since people are content with the apparently beautiful, they identify the really beautiful as a property of things in the sensible world. Accordingly, they are apt to claim for human beings a priority to that property of beauty. Their mistake is in identifying beauty with a property of bodies rather than with the intelligible world. For the allusion to a royal procession, see above 3, 7–20.

12, 30–33 *The explanation for . . . beautiful needs it*: Because persons participate in the One, as does Intellect, the locus of intelligible beauty, people think that they are at least the equals of Intellect and of that which is beautiful.

12, 33–36 *The Good is . . . with the pleasure*: Plotinus here describes the Good in terms used by Agathon in Plato, *Symposium* 196a, 197d to describe *Eros.* One might suppose that Plotinus is correcting Agathon, although at VI.8.15, 1, Plotinus says that the One is "itself lovable and love and love of itself, inasmuch as it is not otherwise beautiful than from itself and in itself." On the idea of the One as love and self-love and its connection with the present passage, see Pigler (2002, 27–74). The amazement and shock occasioned by the encounter with the beautiful is owing to the "forgetting" embodied persons have experienced. Following Plato, Plotinus takes beauty to be the "property" of the Good that attracts us. The amazement and shock is supposed by Plotinus to jolt us back to recognition of our true identity.

12, 36–37 *That which is . . . beautiful is younger*: For those who do not know that beauty is a relational property of the Good, beauty is apt to lead one astray. See VI.7.22, 6–7, where the beautiful becomes "desirable" (*epheton*) when the Good "colors" (*epichōsantos*) it. Of course, the Good is always doing exactly this, but only those who are aware of its existence can see this.

12, 37–39 *The Good is prior . . . all the power*: Dufour takes "in truth" (*tōi alēthei*) as "en realité" on the grounds that it is Intellect, not the One, that contains the truth. But the Good is prior in truth because it is the source of truth for all the Forms. See Plato, *Republic* 508e. The Good's power is "prior" because it is the power of all things.

12, 39–40 *That which comes . . . and from it*: The limitation on the power of Intellect is a function of its complexity or relative absence of oneness. This claim is the inverse of the claim that the infinite power of the One follows from its absolute simplicity (see Commentary 1, 41–43).

12, 40–44 *So, the Good . . . it produced it*: The Good is "sovereign" (*kurios*) over the power of Intellect because it sustains Intellect in existence. The transcendence of the Good is explicated in three points: (a) its removal of all its products from itself, (b) its lack of any need of these, and (c) its identity post production with what it was prior to production. These three characteristics explain why the Good is related to nothing. Yet everything is related to the Good because everything comes from it, is sustained in existence by it, and is fulfilled by approaching it insofar as possible. See Plato, *Philebus* 20d and 67a on the complete self-sufficiency of the Good.

12, 44–45 *This is so . . . be from it*: The Good must be indifferent to the production of anything from it since it is in need of nothing. Yet it does not begrudge anything to its products, including their existence. See V.4.1, 34–36. Cf. Plato, *Timaeus* 29e1–2 where it is the Demiurge that does not begrudge anything to the cosmos he is creating. At *Phaedrus* 247a7, lack of grudging (*aphthonos*) is recognized as a property of divinity generally. This passage makes clear how different is the Plotinian idea of creation from that of the Christian one. The indifference of the Good to its products precludes even the idea of creation as a means to achieving anything by means of creation.

12, 46–47 *As it is . . . come to be*: The account of the nature of the first principle in this treatise entails that there is nothing that could be that is not. If there were such a thing, then the Good would be grudging or limited in some way in exercising its power. This conclusion, named by Arthur Lovejoy the "plenitude of being," applies to the timeless production of Intellect and Soul, including the lowest part of Soul, nature, and matter. It would also seem to apply to the production of the sensible images of the Forms of individuals, that is, to their undescended intellects. The latter point depends on Aristotle's argument that in an everlasting universe all possibilities will at some time be instantiated. See *Metaphysics* 9.4.1047b15ff.

12, 47–50 *But it itself . . . was over them*: Because the Good transcends (*huperbebēkōs*) all things, it can produce all things. I take it that the last clause indicates that the Good sustains everything in existence ("is over them") while at the same time things operate according to their own natures ("leave them to themselves"). See V.2.1, 1–2. Armstrong's translation indicates a different understanding of the last line. He has "but since he transcends all things he can make them and let them exist by themselves while he remains above them." This understanding rejects the claim that the Good is the sustaining cause of the being of everything. This seems contradicted by VI.9.1, 1–2. Besides, if this were so, then we would have to posit for the Good an act of creation and then a withdrawal from the being of its products. The Good's absolute simplicity seems to preclude this. So, too, its lack of any limitation, including self-limitation.

Chapter 13

A final consideration of what the absolute simplicity of the One entails with respect to the possession of properties.

13, 1–2 *But since it . . . of being] good*: We may take this as a reasoned denial of self-predication for the Good. The Good does not even have the property "good" because this would undermine its absolute simplicity. See VI.7.25, 15. The words "have nothing in itself" indicate the Aristotelian use of "in" for predication. The denial of self-predication applies to Forms as well. See VI.4.13, 6–8.

13, 2–6 *For what it . . . it has nothing*: The Good, as primary, cannot be in any sense not good. To be so would compromise its unqualified identity. Yet, it does not have the property of being good. Hence, it has nothing. See VI.7.36, 6ff. on the *via negativa* to the Good. Cf. Alcinous, *Didaskalikos* 165.14ff. (=10.5 Dillon). See the notes in Dillon (1993, 109–110) on the Platonic and Middle Platonic sources for this approach to the first principle.

13, 6–7 *If, then, it . . . from other things*: The words "alone and isolated" are quoted from Plato, *Philebus* 63b7–8. As we have seen (Commentary 5, 22–23 and 9, 34–35), the One is not really related to anything. Its isolation does not set up a real relation as if a "distance" were being erected between entities. The Good is alone because there is nothing outside of or apart from it and because it is absolutely simple. See III.6.9, 37; V.3.10, 17. These two "properties" of the Good are perhaps mutually entailing. Because Aristotle's Unmoved Mover is not, according to Plotinus, absolutely simple, it is false that there cannot be anything apart from it or outside of it.

13, 7–9 *If, then, the . . . by having nothing*: The inference appears to be from the fact that the Good has no properties to the conclusion that it is the Good. Perhaps the implicit reasoning is: That which is without properties is absolutely simple. That which is absolutely simple must be identical with the first principle of all. That which is the first principle of all is the Good, so-called because it is the source of all being and the goal of all desire.

13, 9–11 *If, then, someone . . . that it is*: The "addition" of essence (*ousia*), intellect, or beauty to the first principle of all is a feature of a number of Middle Platonic systems. It is not clear who Plotinus has in mind, but those like Alcinous,

Numenius or Plutarch, for example, quite clearly want to make the first principle of all an intellect of some sort.

13, 11–17 *Therefore, removing everything . . . behind the words*: For the words "removing everything" see the ending of V.3.17, 38. To allow the "is" is to acknowledge the qualified suitability of certain prediction judgments of the Good such as that it is the first principle of all or that it is the source of the being of everything or that it is the goal of all desire. The existential use of "is" is clearly not at issue here. That is, Plotinus is *not* saying that complete accuracy would require us to say that the Good is absolute non-being or nothing but that we can, in a sense, say that it exists. The One does not exist only in the sense in which existence implies compositeness. This passage is a good example of Plotinus applying analysis to figurative or metaphorical language in reference to the Good. When Plotinus himself uses such language, it is always in the context of this analysis.

13, 17–20 *Then, we, too . . . identical to them*: Any "addition" to the Good requires an import of a property or predicative drawn from that which the Good produces and so which is "lesser" than it. The cause of all things, that is, the cause of the being of all things, cannot be identical with any of them. This is another way of saying that that which is autoexplicable must be unique. But because the

Good *is* the cause of all things, it is virtually all things, though not identical with them.

13, 20–23 *For, again, it . . . differentiation is addition*: If the Good were identical with all things, these would have a generic unity, each "thing" being differentiated from another. The same reasoning would apply if the Good were one among many other things. But then the Good would possess a differentiating property, which would be an "addition" to the Good, destroying its simplicity.

13, 23–24 *Then, it would . . . one part good*: The consequence that the Good would be "two" is equivalent to there being a real minor distinction within the Good between it and its differentiating property. Even this minimal sort of complexity is impossible for the first principle of all.

13, 25–27 *Therefore, it will . . . has become good*: The "mixture" (*mikton*) is the supposedly unified composite of "good" plus the differentiating property. Just because the Good, so conceived, would be a composite or mixture, it will not be primarily good. The Good now will be good by participating in the real primary good. The general principle here is that if something is a composite of any sort, then it must participate in its differentiating or distinguishing property. Cf. Plato, *Parmenides* 142c5–7. In that passage, the hypothesized one is one by participating in the essence (*ousia*) of oneness. But here Plotinus adopts the Aristotelian terminology, using the term *diaphora* for the differentiating property. See VI.7.10, 15–17.

13, 27–29 *But, then, the . . . among all things*: If the Good is good by partaking in the Good, then in fact the Good is not one among all things, that is, it is not differentiated from other things by the property of being good.

13, 29–32 *But if the . . . came uniquely good*: The argument for the simplicity of the Good is thus completed. If the Good is good by partaking, that in which it partakes will be the real Good. And this will be necessarily simple; otherwise, there will be a vicious infinite regress in which that which is participated in is not simple but a complex, one part of which is good, and so on.

13, 34–36 *Therefore, that which . . . cause of everything*: Dufour (2006, 183) speculates that this paragraph is an addition by Porphyry, summarizing the argument. See L. Brisson, M.-O. Goulet-Cazé (1982, vol.1, 315–325) for the evidence that in several of the later treatises, Porphyry added such summaries. The Good is "unmixed" (*amiges*) with anything or absolutely simple and "unique" (*monon*). Plotinus actually says "uniquely good" but I take this to indicate its status as first principle, not its nature. Plotinus does not quite infer that it is because it is unmixed and "over everything" that the Good is the cause of all things. What would need to be added would be that the absolutely simple is uncaused or autoexplicable. That the uncaused is the cause of all things follows from the fact that the composite or heteroexplicable must be caused by the autoexplicable. If that were not the case, then the heteroexplicable would in fact be autoexplicable. But it has been shown that the autoexplicable is unique. "Good" here is, then, just the name for that which is simple and unique and so autoexplicable.

13, 36–38 *For neither that . . . is more perfect*: Plotinus (or Porphyry) concludes with the reason for calling the first principle of all "Good." That which is beautiful, namely, all the Forms, and Intellect, cannot come from that which is evil. Nor can they come from that which is indifferent because the product must be inferior to the producer, and the indifferent is inferior to the beautiful. See V.1.7, 37–40; V.2.2, 1–3.

Select Bibliography

I. Ancient Authors

ALCINOUS: Dillon, John. 1993, 1995. *Alcinous: The Handbook of Platonism*. Oxford: Clarendon Press.

ALEXANDER OF APHRODISIAS: Bruns, I., ed. 1887. *De Anima Liber cum Mantissa.* Berlin: Reimer Verlag.

ARISTOTLE: Ross, W. D., ed. 1924. *Aristotle: Metaphysics.* 2 vols. Oxford: Oxford University Press.

———: Ross, W. D., ed. 1949. Aristotle: *Prior and Posterior Analytics*. Oxford: Oxford University Press.

DIOGENES LAERTIUS: Hicks, R. D., trans. 1925, 1991. *Lives of the Eminent Philosophers*. 2 vols. Cambridge, MA: Harvard University Press.

PLATO: Burnet, J., ed. 1900–1907. *Dialogues.* 5 vols. Oxford: Oxford University Press.

PLUTARCH OF CHAERONEA: Paton, W. R., I. Wegehaupt, et al. 1959–1978. *Scripta Moralia*. Leipzig: Teubner Verlag.

PROCLUS: Morrow, G., trans. 1992. *A Commentary on the First Book of Euclid's Elements*. Princeton: Princeton University Press.

———: Tarrant, H. and D. Baltzly. 2007. *Commentary on Plato's* Timaeus. 6 vols. Cambridge, UK: Cambridge University Press.

SEXTUS EMPIRICUS: Bury, R. G., trans. 1905–1924. *Outlines of Pyrrhonism. Against the Professors*. 4 vols. Harvard: Harvard University Press. Vol. 1 contains *Outlines of Pyrrhonism*, vols. 2–5 contain the eleven books known collectively as *Against the Professors*, consisting of Books 1–5: *Against the Logicians* (in vol. 2); *Against the Phycisists* and *Against the Ethicists* (in vol. 3); and Books 6–11, repeating the general title *Against the Professors* (in vol. 4).

Stoicorum Veterum Fragmenta. Von Arnim, H. 1905–1924. 4. vols., Leipzig, 1905-24.

II. Editions and Translations of the *Enneads*

Armstrong, A. H. 1966–1982. *Plotinus*. Greek Text with English Translation and Introductions. Cambridge, MA: Harvard University Press.

Bréhier, E. 1924–1938. *Plotin Ennéades*. Greek Text and French Translation with Introductions and Notes. 7 vols. Paris: Les Belles Lettres.

Brisson, L. and J. P. Pradeau. 2002–2010. *Plotin. Traités*. French Translation and Commentary. 8 vols. Vol. 5 contains treatises 30–37, with a translation and commentary on V.5 by R. Dufour.

Harder, R., R. Beutler, and W. Theiler. 1956–1971. *Plotin*. Greek Text with German Translation and Commentary. 12 vols. Hamburg: Felix Meiner Verlag.

Henry, P. and H.-R. Schwyzer (HS_1). 1951–1973. *Plotini Opera* I–III (editio maior). Bruxelles: Edition Universelle.

Henry, P. H.-R. and Schwyzer (HS_2). 1964–1982. *Plotini Opera* I–III (editio minor, with revised text). Oxford: Clarendon Press.

Igal, J. 1982–1998. *Enéades*. 3 vols. (v. 1.I–II; v. 2.III–IV; v. 3.V–VI.). Madrid: Editorial Gredos.

MacKenna, S. 1962. *Plotinus. The Enneads*. English Translation revised by B. S. Page. London: Faber and Faber.

III. Studies on V.5 and Related Works

Armstrong, A. H. 1960. "The Background to the Doctrine 'That the Intelligibles are not Outside the Intellect.'" In *Les Sources de Plotin*. Geneva: Fondation Hardt, 393–413.

Beierwaltes, W. 1991. *Selbsterkenntnis und Erfahrung der Einheit*. Frankfurt: Vittorio Klostermann.

Bradshaw, D. 2004. *Aristotle East and West. Metaphysics and the Division of Christendom*. Cambridge, UK: Cambridge University Press.

Brisson, L., M.-O. Goulet-Cazé, et al. 1982. *La vie de Plotin*. Vol. 1; 1992. *Porphyre. La vie de Plotin*. Vol. 2. Paris: Librairie Philosophique Vrin.

Charrue, J. M. 1978. *Plotin: Lecteur de Plotin*. Paris: Les Belles Lettres.

Cilento, V. 1971. *Paideia Antignostica. Reconstruzione d'un unico scritto da* Enneadi *III.8, V.8, V.5, II.9*. Florence: Monnier.

Dillon, John M. 1992. "Plotinus and the Chaldaean Oracles." In *Platonism in Late Antiquity*, edited by S. Gersh and C. Kannengiesser. Notre Dame: University of Notre Dame Press, 131–140.

———: 1996. *The Middle Platonists*. 2nd ed. London: Duckworth.

Edwards, M. 1991. "Middle Platonism on the Beautiful and the Good." In *Mnemosyne* 44: 161–167.

Elsas, C. 1975. *Neuplatonische und gnostische Weltablehnung in der Schule Plotins*. Berlin: Walter de Gruyter.

Emilsson, E. 2007. *Plotinus on Intellect*. Oxford: Oxford University Press.

Ferwerda, R. 1982. "Plotinus on Sounds. An Interpretation of Plotinus' *Enneads* V.5.5, 19–27." In *Dionysius* 6: 43–57.

Gerson, L. 2009. *Ancient Epistemology*. Cambridge, UK: Cambridge University Press.

Hadot, P. 1996. "La conception plotinienne de l'identité entre l'intellect et son objet. Plotin et le *De anima* d'Aristote." In *Corps et âme. Sur le* De anima *d'Aristote*, edited by C. Viano. Paris: Librairie Philosophique Vrin, 367–376. Reprinted 1999 in *Plotin, Porphyre: Études néoplatoniciennes*, Paris: Librairie Philosophique Vrin, 267–278.

Harder, R. 1936. "Eine neue Schrift Plotins." In *Hermes* 71: 1–10. Reprinted 1960 in *Kleine Schriften*. Munich, C. H. Beck, 303–313.

Jackson, B. D. 1967. "Plotinus and the *Parmenides*." In *Journal of the History of Philosophy* 5: 315–327.

Kühn, W. 2009. *Quel savoir après le scepticisme*. Paris: Librairie Philosophique Vrin.

Pépin, J. 1956. "Élements pour une histoire de la relation entre l'intelligence et l'intelligible chez Platon et dans le néoplatonisme." In *Revuew philosophique de la France et de l'étranger* 146: 39–64.

Pigler, A. 2002. *Plotin une métaphysique de l'amour*. Paris: Librairie Philosophique Vrin.

Roloff, D. 1970. *Plotin. Die Grossschrift III.8; V.8; V.5; II.9.* Berlin: Walter de Gruyter.

Slaveva-Griffin, S. 2009. *Plotinus on Number.* Oxford: Oxford University Press.

Solmsen, F. 1986. "Plotinus V.5, 3, 21ff., a Passage on Zeus." *Museum Helveticum* 43: 68–73.

IV. General Publications

Armstrong, Arthur H. 1940. *The Architecture of the Intelligible Universe in the Philosophy of Plotinus.* Cambridge: Cambridge Univeristy Press.

Arnou, René. 1968. *Le Désir de Dieu dans la philosophie de Plotin.* 2nd ed. Rome: Presses de l'Université Grégorienne.

Dillon, John M. 1996. *The Middle Platonists.* 2nd ed. London: Duckworth.

Dodds, Eric R., 1965. *Pagan and Christian in an Age of Anxiety.* Cambridge: Cambridge University Press.

Emilsson, Eyjólfur K., 1988. *Plotinus on Sense-Perception.* Cambridge: Cambridge University Press.

———. 2007. *Plotinus on Intellect.* Oxford: The Clarendon Press.

Gerson, Lloyd P. 1994. *Plotinus.* London: Routledge.

———, ed. 1996. *The Cambridge Companion to Plotinus.* Cambridge: Cambridge University Press.

———, ed. 2010. *The Cambridge History of Philosophy in Late Antiquity*. 2 vols. Cambridge: Cambridge University Press.

Hadot, Pierre. 1993. *Plotinus or the Simplicity of Vision*. Translated by M. Chase. Chicago: Chicago University Press.

Inge, W. R. 1948. *The Philosophy of Plotinus*. 3rd ed. London: Longmans, Green.

Lloyd, Anthony C. 1990. *The Anatomy of Neoplatonism*. Oxford: The Clarendon Press.

O'Daly, Gerard J.P., 1973. *Plotinus' Philosophy of the Self*. Shannon, Ireland: Irish University Press.

O'Meara, Dominic J., 1993. *Plotinus: An Introduction to the Enneads*. Oxford: Oxford University Press.

Remes, Pauliina. 2008. *Neoplatonism*. Berkeley: University of California Press.

Rist, John M., 1967. *Plotinus: The Road to Reality*. Cambridge: Cambridge University Press.

Schniewind, Alexandrine. 2003. *L'Éthique du Sage chez Plotin*. Paris: J. Librairie Philosophique Vrin.

Smith. Andrew. 2004. *Philosophy in Late Antiquity*. London: Routledge.

Wallis, Richard T. 1995. *Neoplatonism*. 2nd ed. London: Duckworth.

Index of Ancient Authors

Index of Names and Subjects

• ALSO AVAILABLE FROM PARMENIDES PUBLISHING •

PRE-SOCRATICS

By Being, It Is: *The Thesis of Parmenides* by Néstor-Luis Cordero

Parmenides and the History of Dialectic: *Three Essays* by Scott Austin

Parmenides, Venerable and Awesome: *Proceedings of the International Symposium* edited by Néstor-Luis Cordero

The Fragments of Parmenides: *A Critical Text with Introduction and Translation, the Ancient Testimonia and a Commentary* by A. H. Coxon. Revised and Expanded Edition edited with new Translations by Richard McKirahan and a new Preface by Malcolm Schofield

The Legacy of Parmenides: *Eleatic Monism and Later Presocratic Thought* by Patricia Curd

The Route of Parmenides: *Revised and Expanded Edition, With a New Introduction, Three Supplemental Essays, and an Essay by Gregory Vlastos* by Alexander P. D. Mourelatos

To Think Like God: *Pythagoras and Parmenides. The Origins of Philosophy.* Scholarly and fully annotated edition by Arnold Hermann

The Illustrated To Think Like God: *Pythagoras and Parmenides. The Origins of Philosophy by* Arnold Hermann with over 200 full color illustrations

Presocratics and Plato: *A Festschrift in Honor of Charles Kahn* edited by Richard Patterson, Vassilis Karasmanis, and Arnold Hermann

PLATO

A Stranger's Knowledge: Statesmanship, Philosophy, and Law in Plato's **Statesman** by Xavier Márquez

God and Forms in Plato by Richard D. Mohr

Image and Paradigm in Plato's **Sophist** by David Ambuel

Interpreting Plato's Dialogues by J. Angelo Corlett

One Book, the Whole Universe: *Plato's* Timaeus *Today* edited by Richard D. Mohr and Barbara M. Sattler

Platonic Patterns: *A Collection of Studies* by Holger Thesleff

Plato's Late Ontology: *A Riddle Resolved* by Kenneth M. Sayre

***Plato's* Parmenides:** *Text, Translation & Introductory Essay* by Arnold Hermann. Translation in collaboration with Sylvana Chrysakopoulou with a Foreword by Douglas Hedley

Plato's Universe by Gregory Vlastos

***The Philosopher in Plato's* Statesman** by Mitchell Miller

ARISTOTLE

***One and Many in Aristotle's* Metaphysics**—*Volume 1: Books Alpha-Delta* by Edward C. Halper

***One and Many in Aristotle's* Metaphysics**—*Volume 2: The Central Books* by Edward C. Halper

Reading Aristotle:* Physics *VII.3 "What is Alteration?" *Proceedings of the International ESAP-HYELE Conference* edited by Stefano Maso, Carlo Natali, and Gerhard Seel

HELLENISTIC PHILOSOPHY

A Life Worthy of the Gods: *The Materialist Psychology of Epicurus* by David Konstan

THE *ENNEADS* OF PLOTINUS

With Philosophical Commentaries

Series edited by John M. Dillon and Andrew Smith

Plotinus,* Ennead *IV.8: On the Descent of the Soul into Bodies. *Translation with an Introduction & Commentary* by Barrie Fleet

Plotinus,* Ennead *V.5: That the Intelligibles are not External to the Intellect, and on the Good. *Translation with an Introduction & Commentary* by Lloyd P. Gerson

ETHICS

Sentience and Sensibility: *A Conversation about Moral Philosophy* by Matthew R. Silliman

PHILOSOPHICAL FICTION

Pythagorean Crimes by Tefcros Michaelides

The Aristotle Quest: A Dana McCarter Trilogy. Book 1: Black Market Truth by Sharon M. Kaye

AUDIOBOOKS

The Iliad (unabridged) by Stanley Lombardo

The Odyssey (unabridged) by Stanley Lombardo

The Essential Homer by Stanley Lombardo

The Essential Iliad by Stanley Lombardo

FORTHCOMING

Aristotle's Empiricism: Experience and Mechanics in the Fourth Century B.C. by Jean De Groot

Plato in the Empire: Albinus, Maximus, Apuleius. *Text, Translation, and Commentary* by Ryan C. Fowler

Plotinus, Ennead* I.6: *On Beauty. Translation with an Introduction & Commentary by Andrew Smith

Plotinus, Ennead* II.4: *On Matter. Translation with an Introduction & Commentary by Anthony A. Long

Plotinus, Ennead* II.5: *On What Exists Potentially and What Actually. Translation with an Introduction & Commentary by Cinzia Arruzza

Plotinus, Enneads* IV.3–4, 29: *Problems concerning the Soul. Translation with an Introduction & Commentary by John M. Dillon and Henry Blumenthal

Plotinus, Enneads* IV.1–2, IV.4, 30–45 & IV.5: *Problems concerning the Soul. Translation with an Introduction & Commentary by Gary M. Gurtler

Plotinus, Ennead* IV.7: *On the Immortality of the Soul. Translation with an Introduction & Commentary by Barrie Fleet

Plotinus, Ennead* V.1: *On the Three Principial Hypostases. Translation with an Introduction & Commentary by Eric D. Perl

Plotinus, Ennead* V.8: *On Intelligible Beauty. Translation with an Introduction & Commentary by Andrew Smith

Plotinus, Enneads* VI.4 & VI.5: *On the Presence of Being, One and the Same, Everywhere. Translation with an Introduction & Commentary by Eyjólfur Emilsson and Steven Strange

Plotinus, Ennead* VI.8: *On Free Will and the Will of the One. Translation with an Introduction & Commentary by Kevin Corrigan and John D. Turner